THE GAP DECADE*

*WHEN YOU'RE *TECHNICALLY* AN ADULT BUT REALLY DON'T FEEL LIKE IT YET . . .

KATIE SCHNACK

An imprint of InterVarsity Press
Downers Grove, Illinois

InterVarsity Press
P.O. Box 1400, Downers Grove, IL 60515-1426
ivpress.com
email@ivpress.com

InterVarsity Press® is the book-publishing division of InterVarsity Christian Fellowship/USA®, a movement of students and faculty active on campus at hundreds of universities, colleges, and schools of nursing in the United States of America, and a member movement of the International Fellowship of Evangelical Students. For information about local and regional activities, visit intervarsity.org.

All Scripture quotations, unless otherwise indicated, are taken from The Holy Bible, New International Version®, NIV®. Copyright © 1973, 1978, 1984, 2011 by Biblica, Inc.™ Used by permission of Zondervan. All rights reserved worldwide. www.zondervan.com. The "NIV" and "New International Version" are trademarks registered in the United States Patent and Trademark Office by Biblica, Inc.™

While any stories in this book are true, some names and identifying information may have been changed to protect the privacy of individuals.

Cover design and image composite: David Fassett
Interior design: Daniel van Loon
Images: gold photo: © allierichter7 / pexels-la-miko
  sparse golden confetti: © Anna Efetova / Moment Collection / Getty Images
  abstract star-shaped painting © beastfromeast / DigitalVision Vectors / Getty Images
  glitter gold textured background: © Dimitris66 / DigitalVision Vectors / Getty Images
  rainbow painted abstract: © enjoynz / iStock / Getty Images Plus
  abstract painting of a woman: © muratseyit / E+ / Getty Images

ISBN 978-0-8308-3167-8 (print)
ISBN 978-0-8308-3168-5 (digital)

Printed in the United States of America ∞

InterVarsity Press is committed to ecological stewardship and to the conservation of natural resources in all our operations. This book was printed using sustainably sourced paper.

Library of Congress Cataloging-in-Publication Data
Names: Schnack, Katelyn Marie, 1987- author.
Title: The gap decade : when you're technically an adult but really don't
  feel like it yet / Katie Schnack.
Description: Downers Grove, Il : InterVarsity Press, [2021] | Includes
  bibliographical references.
Identifiers: LCCN 2021025188 (print) | LCCN 2021025189 (ebook) | ISBN
  9780830831678 (print) | ISBN 9780830831685 (digital)
Subjects: LCSH: Young adults—Religious life.
Classification: LCC BV4529.2 .S36 2021 (print) | LCC BV4529.2 (ebook) |
  DDC 248.8/4s—dc23
LC record available at https://lccn.loc.gov/2021025188
LC ebook record available at https://lccn.loc.gov/2021025189

| P | 25 | 24 | 23 | 22 | 21 | 20 | 19 | 18 | 17 | 16 | 15 | 14 | 13 | 12 | 11 | 10 | 9 | 8 | 7 | 6 | 5 | 4 | 3 | 2 | 1 |
| Y | 37 | 36 | 35 | 34 | 33 | 32 | 31 | 30 | 29 | 28 | 27 | 26 | 25 | 24 | 23 | 22 | 21 |

FOR KYLE, SUNNY, AND SHEPHERD

CONTENTS

MIND THE GAP

Getting old is weird. Especially when you are expected to act, feel, and behave like a "real adult," but inside you are still pretty convinced you are just a confused youth. Perhaps a youth who is now growing a couple forehead wrinkles but still unsure about this great big world we are expected to function in. This strange period of time starts in your twenties and continues until at least early thirties. Possibly even far beyond, but I can't really say because I am still in my early thirties and am not very psychic.

Taking a "gap year" has become a popular thing to do. This is where the young humans of the world take a sort of sabbatical before or after college to just, well, enjoy life and think about their next step for a hot minute. It is almost like an Amish rumspringa, without the Amish part and likely not involving a horse and buggy. But what about a gap decade?

Let's talk about that, because it's something we *all* walk through, but not by choice. A gap decade isn't a cute whim of a decision to take a pause and travel to Italy for a few months. Nah. A gap decade is a cluster of challenging, transitional years that the universe just dumps in your lap. And my lap. And pretty much everyone's lap. It's that twilight zone between "young person" and "full-blown adult" that sort of washes in, bringing with it a bit of chaos, growth, and self-discovery. It is a few years of flailing around, trying to figure out what the heck is happening as you move from not old to kinda old. From young adult to adult adult.

This book walks through that season of my life. My own experience with the gap decade. But it isn't just about my story, folks. This book tackles universal issues and emotions we all face— loneliness, change, grief, laughter, relationships, faith, and more. I hope these words make you feel seen and less alone as you read them. I hope by me sharing (with brutal honesty, even when it's awkward to do so) about my experiences, you can feel more comfortable about your own. It is as simple as that. Books I've read in the past that made me say, "Wow—I thought I was the only one!" have made such an impact on my life. I hope this book does that for you. Or at least just makes you laugh, because humor makes everything a little bit better.

Love,

Katie

PART ONE

THE WAITING GAME

Hey there. You know what's hard? Waiting. And yes, even waiting for things like your coffee to brew is really tough. HURRY UP, YOU SLOW DRIPPING MONSTER OF AGONY. But I am talking about waiting in a dry, gut-wrenching season of life. Ya feel me? A season that makes you go, "I am here. But I *really* want to be over *there*, but I have zero idea how that will happen or if it even will." Times of waiting and wanting can come at any stage of life—waiting for the right job to come along. Waiting for a spouse. Waiting for that baby to come along. Waiting for a new juicy true crime documentary to release on Netflix. It can get hard, guys. The wait is hard.

Learning how to be at peace in the waiting is tough, but if you can master it, it will be invaluable. I hope you know God is there in the waiting, even when it seems like he instead took a vacation to Maui. God is there, seeing you wait, feeling your heartbreak and whispering to you, "Just keep holding on a bit longer. I know what I am doing."

The first part of this book is about one of my first big seasons of waiting. One where I didn't know what was next, how things were going to work out, or even what step to take, and it was scary. But, hey—I made it through. You will too.

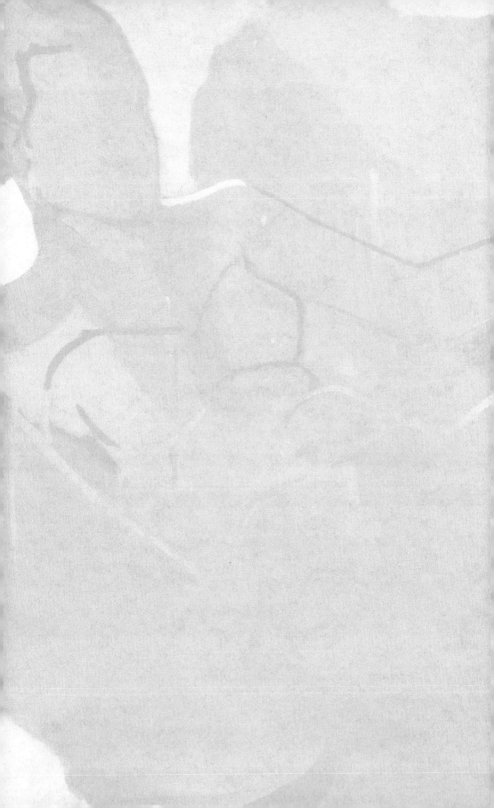

CHAPTER ONE

SEASONS OF WAITING ARE HARD

Something really crazy happened to me when I was twelve. I met my husband, Kyle. And, even as a lanky preteen whose thinking was typically tainted by the constant cloud of Bath and Body Works Cucumber Melon body spray fumes I lived within, I knew the moment I saw him we were meant to be together, with a sense of clarity and complete peace. I knew he was my person. My lobster. Whatever you want to call it. Wild, right? And of course very cheesy. But there ya have it, folks. My love origination story is one big ball of cheese.

We were at a birthday party in our suburban Minnesota town. It was spring, and the air still had that damp chill to it yet was full of new life. Everyone seemed to be buzzing off the energy of knowing the snow was finally gone for good and summer was right around the corner. I was wearing the ugliest bright red hoodie possible with our high school logo on it—go Cardinals. Kyle was wearing a Hawaiian shirt and khaki cargo pants with pockets big enough to store a Nokia cell phone *and* a Walkman, which is very impressive. My hair was "scrunched" with so much Suave hairspray. Every natural curl was shellacked tight and secure, as it could only be in 1999. Kyle's hair was bleached "blond," but it looked orange because that is what happens when a teenage boy does at-home highlights. It was plastered with so much product it stuck straight up to the heavens in spikes sharp enough to poke out multiple eyeballs at once.

I remember thinking how cute Kyle was. I remember how good he smelled—must have been all that hair gel. I remember every detail about that otherwise inconspicuous party—how my friend pierced her own tongue right there in the basement and I thought it was cool. (WHAT?) How we did a whole lot of nothing but it was just fun to be with each other. I remember the grass was so green and thick, and the sky was cloudy but the wind was calm. I remember the feeling in my stomach when I bounced on the trampoline in my friend's yard and when I looked at *him*— Kyle, my husband-to-be.

And yes, he was cute and all, but I think the part that really made him stand out to me as a prime choice in a future mate was when I accidentally spilled my can of Coke. Being the forever messy, way-too-fast-moving person that I am, I just put a phone book over the spill and continued on with my life. (ALSO, WHAT?) A minute later I looked back and saw he was cleaning up my mess with a dishrag. And yes, he has been doing so ever since, if you must know.

Late that night under the dark Minnesota sky and orange glow of a street lamp, Kyle asked me to be his girlfriend, because that is the cringeworthy question you ask when you are twelve. My answer was no, because clearly I was a progressive young woman and I need to *actually know* a person before signing up for such a serious commitment. My goodness, preteen Katie. Chill.

Five days later we went to a movie and barely spoke to each other the entire night. But before our parents rolled up to take us home, he asked again. Apparently, our near-silent movie date was enough for me, and I said yes.

We stayed together all throughout high school. I kept waiting to get sick of him, or for us to grow apart, but it never happened. We only grew closer. Nobody could make me laugh as much as he did, and everything was so *easy* with him. He made me really happy; it was as simple as that. I didn't have a lot of experience with love, but I knew what I felt, and it felt real.

But life has ups and downs, and unfortunately being a kid doesn't shield you from that. Part of the reason we got so serious so fast was that we were forced to deal with some tough stuff really early on. When we were sixteen, Kyle's dad became very sick for several months and eventually died. Hospital visits, weepy phone calls, funerals, and navigating life after tragedy became part of our story. Then about a year later, Kyle collapsed at my house and was rushed to the emergency room. He had to have major surgery on his stomach and was in the hospital for weeks. I remember his terrible hospital breath, those hideous tan socks with the grippy bottoms the nurses put on him, and curling up with him in the bed as the tiny TV hanging from the ceiling quietly played in the background. My love for him during that time ran so, so deep. I was so worried about him and so in love with him. And so sick of hospitals. We were not even eighteen yet.

During our senior year of high school, we decided to go to separate colleges in the fall. Okay fine, I'll admit it! It was my stupid idea. Even though I loved him, I felt we had to be "rational." What did we really know about true love, right? We were still kids! We needed space. Right? Isn't that what they say in movies? Space? Even though part of my brain knew it was true, I refused to believe I actually found my soulmate at a random birthday party when I was twelve. Things like that don't happen. I was basically asking God to prove to me this beautiful, amazing gift he had given me was actually real, and I did that by returning the gift to the store for a bit, which makes no sense.

So, off we went, me to school in West Palm Beach, Florida, and him to Sioux Falls, South Dakota, which he hated. I mean, can you blame him? I had the beach, and he had a lot of roaming buffalos. It wasn't a fair split. That year was hard, as we were living thousands of miles apart. We didn't even have FaceTime then, and we could send about four texts a day before getting charged overage fees. We were living in the long-distance relationship stone age, and it wasn't working. So, we broke up. I guess we dated other people that year but . . . let's pretend we didn't and just not discuss that part. Yikes. It was all one dark, hot mess.

Then, things got even more complicated. That year I had made the most amazing best friend, Jenna, then tragically lost her in a car crash the day she was driving home for the summer.

The day after she died I flew back to Minnesota, and Kyle was waiting for me at the airport with my parents. I can still remember the looks on their faces as I descended the escalator toward them. Calm, placid, and bursting with worry just below the surface. Even though I had been pretty awful to him all year long, broken his heart, and ended something really good we had together, Kyle was there, handing me flowers, walking with me silently to the car, as he knew more than anyone there was nothing he could say to me to make anything better. That night he held me on the couch as I sobbed, and then every night that summer as the tears continued to fall. We were back together again right then, and we didn't even really need to discuss it. We just knew. And, we would never be apart again.

The next year Kyle joined me at my school in Florida. He grew his hair long and instantly became tan with his olive Danish skin. He began surfing and was once hit by a shark in the leg. We made all the same friends and worked together at the same swanky hotel serving mini crab cakes and caviar to socialites. We studied—I guess? It's all a college blur. But mostly, we enjoyed being near each other again in the same state, the same life. Together, wrapped up tighter than ever before.

The older we got, the more interesting of a person he became to me. He was majoring in theater and could memorize entire scripts of Shakespeare in one sitting. He wore torn, dirty jeans— not as a fashion statement but just because he only owned one pair of jeans and wore them so much until they naturally became stylish. He sang Frank Sinatra and blared horrible musical theater cast recordings that made me want to rip my ears off but lit him up. Then he would jam out to Garth Brooks and rap every single word to Eminem. He got the most random tattoos—a bear with antlers growing out of it and a flock of bats flying out of his armpit. That one was on sale—only $13, a Friday the Thirteenth special. I love anything cheap, including permanent body art. Kyle was so random and odd in the best ways yet also levelheaded where it mattered. We fit together even as we got older, just like we had from the beginning.

So, with all that drama and joy, heartache and tough stuff, tied up with the love we had for each other, it didn't feel weird when he proposed at the age of nineteen. NINETEEN, PEOPLE. Yes, now I realize how ridiculous and young that is. But then again, maybe it isn't. Hard to say. We felt like we had already lived through so much together and knew there was nothing we couldn't handle together in the future. And even more so, there wasn't anything we *wanted* to face without the other one by our side. We couldn't see our life without each other in it.

We got married at twenty-one, a few weeks after his birthday so he could legally drink champagne at the reception. Total babies. We wed in Minnesota in an old church next to a lake and then danced the night away at a quirky, musty country club with loud carpet and a million antique paintings hanging on the wall. High on a hill, overlooking the skyline of St. Paul, we celebrated with everyone we loved, and it was perfect. We felt perfect.

Life does this sometimes. It brings times of cutting heartache, sure, but then also times of pure joy. Easy, fun, beautiful seasons of life are not just a mythical unicorn, I promise. They do exist. It is easy to put a lot of focus on the hard times, but good times come around eventually. There are those moments when you look around and realize today, now, right here, things are just *good*. I have learned to savor those seasons, because they are equally as important and truthful as the hard ones.

After getting married, Kyle and I still had college to finish— one year for me, two for him. A victory lap! Turns out he surfed a bit *too* much that year he transferred down and had to retake some classes, and not all his credits came through from his first year in South Dakota. But I still blame the surfing. So, we moved into our campus married housing and began our life as husband-and-wife college students.

Our first home was a three-hundred-square-foot old converted garage with only two windows, one of them mostly taken up by an air conditioner unit. It was nestled under a huge mango tree and had that musty, old Florida smell to it. Sweet and swampy all at once. The house was so small I would joke that I could sit on my couch and make dinner at the same time, which would almost be true if I had gigantic arms. Our table folded out from the wall, and then we folded it back in when we were done, and only one of us could fit in the bathroom at a time. To us, it was perfect. Our own mini piece of paradise, just for the two of us.

I know the first year of marriage is supposed to be hard, but since we got married so young and were still in college, we were shielded from a lot of the tough, true-life adult stuff that hits you after you graduate and several years after that. Things were still set up for us like college kids. We had health insurance through our school. I think our rent for our hut-disguised-as-a-home was about $3 a month. We didn't have to pay our student loans back yet. We were both working—both still serving socialites at our college job, and then I had my first post-college job at the local news station, running cameras for the morning show. We had an awesome group of friends still surrounding us. We loved our church that we had been at for years. We had security, community, and each other. It felt like the most blissful way to enter into marriage. We were adults but still living in a college world, and we loved every minute of it together.

But we knew we couldn't hide in our little mango-covered nest forever. Eventually, the universe would kick us out and force us to face actual adulthood and purchase our own fruit from a store, not pick it from out our window. Kyle began applying for graduate schools to get an MFA in acting. We were looking at programs all across the country, all of them in cities we had never even been to before and where we didn't know anybody. It was exciting and terrifying all at once.

We had no idea what the next year of our life would look like, what state we would live in, or if Kyle would even get into school, which brought a whole second set of worries along. We were in one of those suspended twilight zone times where you know everything is about to change, but you don't exactly know how, why, or even when, which can be the most difficult part. But change was coming, we could feel it. The reality of that began to blanket our days with the wondering, worrying, and wanting. And while we yearned in our guts for easy and quick answers to what was next, we had to wait. This was a full-blown adult 101 lesson for us: figuring out how to wait for something big without losing your mind in the process. Everything we knew and had grown to be comfortable with was about to be flipped in an entirely new direction, yet we didn't know if it would be up, down, east, or west. I wanted control over our destiny, but that wasn't possible, so we waited. And waiting is really hard.

It's hard when your heart wants to be ten steps ahead of where you are but you have zero idea how to get there, or where *there* even is. Waiting seasons can be agonizing, especially for people like me who are action-takers and want to quickly fix things and only feel good feelings along the way. Often, during these times of having to wait, it seems like God is silent, not listening, out to lunch. Because if he *wasn't*, wouldn't he be hearing our daily desperate prayers for an answer, for a change, for some sort of clarity, and our season of waiting would be OVER WITH BY NOW?

But of course, that isn't how things work. God isn't Amazon Prime. But I do think he knows a few more things than Jeff Bezos, so I am okay with trusting in his time schedule. Well, at least I try to be.

Over the next few years, Kyle and I would walk through several more long periods of waiting. Waiting to find out where our next move would be. Waiting to find if we would get the job, or any job for that matter. Waiting to find if we would have enough money. Waiting for new friends to come. Waiting for answers, for darkness to lift, for resolutions. Just a lot of waiting. After college and through your twenties and thirties, there is a lot of uncertainty. So much effort and energy is put into trying to acquire things, figure things out, and get to the next page of your story when you just wish you could read the last chapter first to know how it is all going to end.

Now, looking back on the times when we felt we were running a marathon though we would have much preferred to take an Uber, it is easy to see how God was there all along. Every morning, he was there. In every anxious, mundane moment, he was there, whispering to me, "Hold on. I know what I am doing. My timing is perfect. I love you, and I have this figured out. Just trust me." Sometimes I just forgot to listen for that whisper, but even then, it was still there.

I have seen in my life, and do believe with my whole heart, that if nothing else—if no fast answers are available, no quick fixes, no signs and wonders flashing in your face—God will in those moments give us enough to simply get through the day, if we ask him. And then get through the next, and the next, until we can finally see the light at the end of the tunnel and know our season of waiting is about to end. Because it does end.

So, for Kyle and me, as we sat in our little garage house and tried to understand what the next decade of our life would look like, where it would bring us, and how we would survive, we fought hard to not think about everything we didn't know and to focus on what we did. We had each other. We had joy that most days overtook our anxious thoughts. We had faith, though imperfect and evolving. And, for now, that was enough.

CHAPTER TWO

WHILE YOU WAIT, EAT NACHOS AND HUG YOUR FRIENDS

I walked into a restaurant and an entire table of my friends started cheering and then chanting: *"Drama! Drama! Drama!"* In response, I did a very Fresh Prince Carlton–worthy dance move to solidify the moment in all its absurdity. Apparently I had a nickname. And apparently these people thought I was a bit "extra" as a human being, so Drama it was. But the ironic thing: every single one of them was a theatre major, yet I was the one who was considered dramatic. Go figure. But guess what? They could call me anything they wanted because they were *my people* and it felt good to have then in my life. Because having a group that chants nicknames when you enter the room isn't a guarantee. In fact, it is a rare gift. Good friends are hard to come by, and I knew that, so I was soaking up those moments with them.

The chanting and weird dance moves in reciprocation happened every Monday. We would gather at our favorite grimy, beach-themed restaurant to eat, drink, and be merry. We crowded closely around a few tables pushed together, probably making other patrons slightly annoyed at our loud storytelling and laughter. But the laughter was the best part. During those nights there were two things we could count on: a lot of jokes and a lot of nachos. And that is a beautiful thing.

After college, and as you get deeper into your twenties and beyond, it seems like one of the biggest things that change is friendships. And it kind of hurts, in the way getting smacked in the face with a giant frozen salmon unexpectedly hurts. It catches you off guard, is confusing and painful, and flat-out stinks all at once. After graduation, people move away, become consumed by their jobs, get married, go overseas, or decide they now prefer Netflix and hiding under a cluster of cats instead of running around downtown late into the weekend nights like their wayward years of the past. And yes, change is good, of course. Bring it on! Because a fifty-five-year-old probably shouldn't have the same weekend agenda as a twenty-one-year-old. At least not often. Maybe once a year, or twice if they work out. But also, loneliness is a real, harsh thing, and as you get older it can get tough to fight that off. Boo! Lame! Loneliness sucks. Yet I know we all experience it, which is a bit strange. If we are all feeling it, why don't we all do something to *fix* it, together? Ya know, so we are not . . . lonely anymore?

For example, when I was working on a writing project once, I gathered my closest girlfriends at the time so they could read it, give me feedback, and brainstorm other ideas that were relevant to our lives at the moment. I had them all show up at my co-working space, I stuffed them full of mimosas and bagels, and we laughed and read and discussed. It was a really special morning for me, as these women took time out of their lives and simply showed up to help, and I felt so blessed by that. As I looked around the table, I was grateful to have so many women I could call on and who also called on me back. But then when I asked the question, "What is one of the hardest parts of getting older for you?" guess what the majority of those women said. Loneliness. Which, in a way, surprised me because we were all sitting together, dining together, sharing our lives with each other in that exact moment. But how often did we make this intentional time for each other? Apparently not enough, because we all felt the sting of loneliness in our hearts. We all yearned to have more people around us who made our souls light up like the mom's living room in *Stranger Things*. In our day-to-day lives, we needed more than just Carl, our cubicle neighbor who always had a dry tickle in his throat and chewed gum too loud. Carl wasn't cutting it.

There is deep beauty in genuine community and friendships that feel like family. In fact, God straight up instructs us to have friends. In the Bible, God urges us to meet with and encourage each other.[1]

I find it funny how God has to forcefully spoon-feed us the good things in life sometimes. Ugh, fine, I will find people I like, spend time with them, and then be chill on Sundays. If you insist.

But guess what? No matter if you are twenty, thirty, or ninety, it is possible to make room for people in your life. (After one hundred it may get dicey, as likely you both won't be able to hear each other speak.) So, if you are in a state of perpetual loneliness, I hope you know that a lot of other people around you are as well. Sometimes someone just has to make the first move.

---

[1]Hebrews 10:24-25. And this concludes the only normal footnote in the whole book. All others will just be weird.

The year of the Monday night nachos was such a great example of friendship and community. It was right after I graduated college, and Kyle was still finishing up his remaining few credits as he applied to grad school. We were waiting for our next step, and our life was full of school, work, and friends. I was busy with my new job. I drove myself to work at 3:30 a.m. to be ready for the 5:00 a.m. newscast, fueled by bad coffee, passion for journalism, and a determination to climb the ladder. Any ladder, really. I was new to this whole working thing. Soon I was promoted to associate producer. Did I know what that meant at the time? Nope, but I knew it sounded cool, and so I began my first foray into the art of "faking it until you make it." With that promotion, I was moved from the morning shift to the night shift. The coffee got better as I sipped it slowly between evening shows while cracking jokes with the news anchor about his pet monkey. We had our last show at 10:00 p.m., and I was out the door by 10:31.

On Mondays, I would head straight from work to the restaurant, where I would find Kyle already one plate of nachos deep and likely ordering his second, surrounded by our friends and the big plaster mermaid adorning the dark wood walls.

We went there on Monday nights because the restaurant held a promotion. If you bought a pitcher of soda or beer, you got a free plate of nachos. Say no more. Sign me up. The best part was the free "plate" was closer to the size of a small island nation. A mound of the most salty, perfect tortilla chips, a heap of dairy products that would put a shiver through even the spine of a Nebraska cow farmer, and a mountain of guacamole. And this was even before avocados became so *trendy*. Back then, it was just normal guac.

But surrounding the haystacks of cheese and chips was a circle of friends we had known and loved for years, and that is really what brought us there every week. They were the type of friends who felt more like family, having lived through so many days and nights and nacho plates together. It was all so comfortable and easy. We always had the same waitress and always sat at the same table in the back, under that stupid mermaid statue, which would, without fail, provoke outbreaks of the song "Under the Sea" by the theatrical crew. And yes, every Monday, as dependable as the cheese bloat we would all have the next morning, they would chant the name Drama as I walked in. It was the perfect way to kick off a week: nachos, nicknames, and mermaids. Thank you, Jesus.

We didn't know it at the time, but as we got older these sweet moments of community would become fewer and further between. There would be seasons where Kyle and I only had each other, our pets, and the Roku remote to spend our weekend with. There would be seasons where we were trapped by demanding jobs and teething babies and it felt like we would never exit our own home again without being weighed down by a diaper bag and covered in spit-up bananas.

But guess what? True, real community and friends—like the ones we would share nachos with every single week—are not only something reserved for those under the age of twenty-five. That is a lie the demons of adulthood like to whisper in our ears. Not today, lame-o Satan. Friends and community are still obtainable at any age. You just have to work a little harder for it.

One year, after two cross-country moves away from Florida and that restaurant with the tacky mermaid, I was so sick of feeling lonely. I wanted *people* again in my life, and I was ready to do something drastic to get them. No, I wasn't planning on kidnapping and creating an underground bunker like in *Unbreakable Kimmy Schmidt.* I wasn't that desperate. But I did get real awkward and uncomfortable as I intentionally set out on a quest to make community. Because even feeling awkward is better than feeling lonely.

Kyle and I had planned to go camping one weekend, and instead of going by ourselves I decided to invite everyone we kinda sorta knew at the time to join us, and then a few people I didn't know. Hey—I met you about three-and-a-half times at church! Come sleep in the wilderness with us? Friends of friends are of course welcome. I even invited a girl I ran into at a coffee shop who I had only met once before. I was the one who extended the first hand, made the first move at the risk of looking like a dork, and hoped people would reciprocate. Guess what? They did. People said yes. Even the coffee shop girl said yes. A lot of people said yes, actually.

I realized that if Kyle and I were feeling lonely and not exactly loving it, there was a strong chance others were feeling the same thing. Just like my girlfriends around our conference table full of bagels—we were all feeling it. We just needed to do something about it.

Did it feel weird asking people we didn't know very well to come take a trip with us? Absolutely. But it was better than the alternative of staring at the campfire by ourselves and drinking warm red wine alone and feeling sad about it. So that weekend a caravan of people left the comforts of the city for the lakeside wilderness and set up tents under the shade of the trees to the soundtrack of cicadas. As we were getting settled, some of the girls we were with started happily yelling, and I looked over to see them hugging someone in the campground next to them. They knew her! That girl had no idea we were going to be there; she had decided to just go solo camping for the weekend. She literally had snagged the very last site in the whole park, and it was right next to us—all of us. A whole big gaggle of people she was now forced to be with, all weekend long, and the poor girl was a total introvert. At least before we showed up and forced her into socialization.

Perhaps this was God giving her what she needed instead of what she *thought* she needed. Or maybe she wanted to be surrounded by a bunch of friends and didn't know how to get there, which makes sense—I'm sure many people can relate to that. Not everybody is a loud extrovert asking a coffee-shop passerby to come sleep in a tent. I would love to think that this girl found herself lonely like we all do every now and again, then prayed about it, went solo camping, and BAM. There we were. But perhaps she really was just looking forward to a quiet weekend in the woods and got the exact opposite. Either way, we had a great time.

So there we were, a ragtag group of people who didn't know each other all that well, forcing ourselves into making inside jokes and new nicknames and memories that eventually cemented us together for a long time after that. We made the choice to choose community and people and fun and friendships over the easier route of isolation and weekends spent alone binging on whatever new murder documentary was streaming. And even though the camping trip didn't include free nachos, it did create relationships that would last for years. It gave me people again.

For me, having friends brings so much light to my life. I know everyone needs different levels of social interaction, which is of course fine, but it goes beyond enjoying yourself at a barbecue or secretly hating every second of it. There is an important middle ground. Having people you can count on like family—and who you may even like a bit better than your own family—is such a gift and so needed. As you get older, it's easy to get stuck in patterns of sameness, responsibilities, and doing things solo. But aging isn't a death sentence. (Well kind of, but you get it.) We still have a choice to show up and have fun along the way. And while I don't eat nachos or drink cheap beer every Monday now (hi, gluten allergy), I do still fight to make time for friends between all the less-fun stuff being an adult brings about. And I hope even when I am ninety-five I will continue to do so. I hope I will forever choose the uncomfortable way of life that involves putting myself out there and making the room and time to cultivate relationships. Soaking it all up. Squeezing as much joy out of this existence as possible. Getting vulnerable all in the name of making life a bit sweeter, a bit more fun, and a bit fuller of people that I love.

During that year of nachos and friends, my heart was often looking forward to where we would be next as I anxiously awaited the new adventure that I knew was just on the horizon. But looking back now, I can see that while I waited, I was so lucky to have people around me and so much joy to get me through. The day came, yes, when we finally knew where we were headed for Kyle's graduate program—the University of Texas at Austin. But before we finally had that clarity, I am glad I had so many plates of nachos with so many beautiful people. Because that is something to be cherished.

PART TWO

#WERK

Hey there. Oh, work. Or #werk. It is more fun to spell it that way. This part tackles that time in life when you are hustling, trying, wanting, hoping for the perfect job, career, CALLING to appear. We are so used to things being instantaneous these days. I order groceries on my phone,[1] and they show up in less than two hours. But some things in life are bigger than a fresh twelve-pack of La Croix showing up at your doorstep in record time. Some things, like figuring out what you want to "do with your life," or how the literal heck you are going to take the steps to get there, take longer. And that is okay. And if you are not living your dream career by twenty-five or thirty-five or even fifty-five, that is okay also. As long as you keep listening to your heart, take brave leaps into the unknown, and strive for a life you love—however that may look—you are killing it.

---

[1] Usually from the bathroom. And that, my friends, is my TED Talk on efficiency.

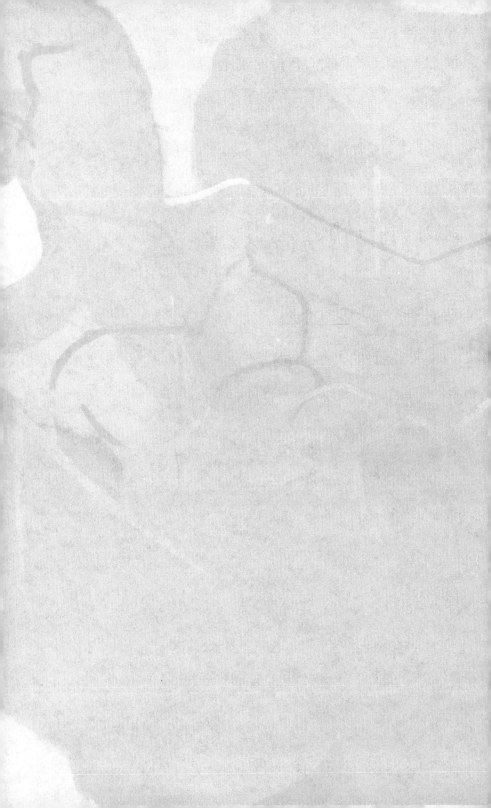

CHAPTER THREE

IT IS OKAY TO CHANGE YOUR MIND. IT IS NOT OKAY TO THROW A STAPLER ACROSS THE OFFICE

My boss, Carol,[1] an early-fifties woman with a tuft of short, bleached hair and frizzy, teased bangs, was freaking out. It appeared she had lost her mind, judging by her thrashing and repetitive screaming of "I quit! I quit! I can't take it anymore! I quit!" in the middle of the newsroom, her face as red as an organic beet, which is a distinctly different shade of red than a normal beet. And the woman wasn't kidding either—she really *was* quitting, in the most dramatic, should-be-posted-on-YouTube way. She frantically gathered things off her desk, threw a stapler out of her cubicle, grabbed her keys, and ran out the door. There was one slight issue that made this pearl-clasping work storm-out even more shocking: she was the executive producer of the 6:00 p.m. newscast. It was currently 5:52, and our captain had abandoned the ship.

---

[1]Name has been changed to protect the angry. But you get it. She had a strong "Carol" vibe.

It was now about a year after I had graduated college. I had been uprooted from lowly camera operator to a bit less lowly associate producer. I moved from the morning news to the night and worked evenings when Kyle was typically at rehearsal anyway. At first, the job was everything I thought I wanted. I was chasing down dramatic stories, interviewing questionable citizens of the community, and frantically sprinting through the newsroom in high heels because running in high heels makes a woman feel *powerful.*

One of my first few days as a producer, with just minutes until we went to air, Carol stood up and screamed, "Michael Jackson died!" She whipped around and looked me straight in the eyes, dramatically pointed at me with one shaky finger, and yelled, "You. Go to the file room and get stock footage of him, *now!*" Well, first of all, I didn't know where the file room was yet, so there was that problem. Second—come again? Do what now and where? Luckily, I am always up for a challenge and am apparently fine learning things with a two-minute-and-thirty-second deadline. So I grabbed a photographer who had worked there awhile, and we sprinted back to the large room full of old tapes (oh, that is where it is—good to know), found the one with Michael Jackson on it, and made it all happen in time for the show to open.

That is basically what it was like working in TV news. Ridiculous, random things would happen, and you would flail around for a few seconds but then always get your job done on a deadline of mere minutes. Somehow, someway, you made it happen, even with only seconds to spare. The adrenaline of that was fun, and it was all fine and great. Well, until it just wasn't.

In the early months of my job, all the death, doom, and destruction of the news didn't get to me too much. Hey—it's journalism! I knew what I was getting into. And there were a lot of positive stories we reported on as well, buried beneath the chaos sure, but they were there. But after a while of day in and day out writing and thinking about crime and natural disasters and politics and tough, sad subjects, I guess I remembered I had a soul. It all began to feel a little too dark for a forty-hour work week, month after month. It began to chip at me, slowly but steadily. For example, one day there was a silver alert out for a missing elderly woman. Poor lil' old Granny Toots, where art thou? We had scheduled it as the leading story of our show. But before we went to air, Granny Toots was found safe. My coworker yelled out in frustration, "Dang it! They found that old lady!" A safely found grandma isn't news, I guess.

Then the doom and destruction hit even closer to home when some of my coworker's family members were killed in a shooting, including his sweet little daughter. We were all devastated. The killer was on the loose for weeks, and I was the one who answered the phone when my coworker called to tell us they finally caught him hiding out in some nondescript motel in the Florida Keys.

But the last straw for me was the 2010 Haiti earthquake, where more than 250,000 people died. When that happened, it was days and days of me editing video clips to make sure we didn't put any dead bodies on air. The viewers didn't see them, but I did, every night, and it broke my heart.

After the earthquake coverage, I felt that stirring, that feeling that says, *Not this, something else.* There is something else for you. But that something else is usually a big dark question mark. You know it's there, somewhere out in the universe, but you don't know where, what it looks like, or how to even begin searching.

A few weeks before Carol had her meltdown, Kyle was accepted into a graduate program in Austin, Texas. Finally, we had a bit of an answer about what would be next for us, and Kyle had three years ahead of him to learn more about his art and get paid in the process. We would be in a brand-new state and have a fresh place to start over in any way we wanted to. I had been handed a blank slate only a year after grabbing my diploma. I had the opportunity to decide if working in the news was the path I wanted to keep going down. I knew it wasn't, but I wasn't sure what was.

Then one day it became clear to me what drew me to journalism in the first place. I was back home in Minnesota for a vacation and was watching my dad around a campfire waving his hands and telling us a dramatic tale about a recent Sasquatch sighting near my cabin. Yes, clarity came through Sasquatch. It wasn't that I yearned for a helmet of perfectly shellacked bleached blond news reporter hair and a Velveeta Cheese–smooth news reporter voice and my own booth at the state fair. What I wanted was to tell good stories. I wanted to make people laugh, keep them entertained. I wanted to write, and write something longer than a thirty-second script on today's city council meeting or who murdered who last night. Those were not the stories I wanted to put into the universe. I wanted to make people feel seen, less alone, and to laugh a little bit along the way. I wanted to write books like the ones I cherished and read every week that helped me grow, learn, and expand myself, my mind, my worldviews, and my faith.

It made sense I would want this as a career. For one, I had my dad, who frequently told dramatic tales about that pesky local 'squatch, or the aliens who live at the bottom of the ocean, or that one time he caught a fish the size of a small elephant but conveniently didn't have a camera to capture the moment. He was a storyteller in his own way and had always been one. Also, I have loved reading my entire life. My mom would take me to the library every week as a child and we would load up on a dozen books, and I would read through them all. No Boxcar Children or Goosebumps plot could hold me back.[2] When I was even younger, I was drawing picture books and writing little lines of text, then shoving them at my mom begging her to call a publisher, because, of course, it is that easy.

And yes, this is one of those cute, eye-roll-worthy yet valid little quips. If you don't know what you want to do with your life, think about what you loved as a child and start there. And there is your serving of Basic Becky self-help advice for the day. But cheesy or not, it worked for me. Ten out of ten would recommend revisiting your childhood passions if you are trying to figure out what to do as an adult that makes your insides sparkle like a rhinestone cowboy on dollar beer nights at the honky tonk.

Circling back to my boss who completely lost her crap in the middle of the newsroom. The day after her freak-out, she showed up at work with her chin held high like nothing ever happened, turned in her two-week notice to HR, and sat at her desk to finish her job. You had to commend her for that. That week I also turned in my two-week notice for our move to Texas, but in a much calmer fashion. I didn't even throw a single piece of office equipment across the room and had zero veins popping out of my forehead. Boring.

When Carol heard I was also leaving, she walked over to my cubicle and leaned on the ledge. "Congrats on the move," she said, her eyes calm. "Are you going to keep working in TV news when you get to Austin?"

---

[2]Except for the Goosebumps book about the ventriloquist doll that comes to life. That crap still scares me to this day.

"No, I'm not planning on it," I said. "It was interesting and such a fun first job out of college, but definitely not what I wanted to do for the rest of my life."

She was staring right at my face but seemed to be looking right through me into the depths of her bleak future. That or she had indigestion. Hard to say.

"Man," she sighed. "I wish I had the courage to make that choice twenty-five years ago," she said, her forehead wrinkling just a little. "Now here I am, miserable. I don't know what to do next, and I don't know what is left for me." She walked away abruptly. Which was good, because I had no advice or even a remotely comforting quip to give her. That was some deep stuff and awkwardly honest for our previously very professional and curt relationship. I'm pretty sure the most words she had said to me at this point was when she screamed at me to go find old video of Michael doing the moonwalk.

But what she said echoed through me. Because if I didn't take this opportunity to make my own U-turn and find what I really wanted to focus on as a career, I knew it would only get more complicated to do so. Not impossible, but more complicated. I knew I was at a crossroads—continue down the path I was already on, which was comfortable and easy but just a wee bit soul crushing. Or I could take a step into the vast unknown and find a path that was a better fit. Do what was "safe," or venture out to find something that put a little salsa in my pants and made me cha cha down the church aisles.[3]

But simply saying "Chase those dreams!" is cheap and easy. Cool advice, bro. Slap it on a V-neck and sell it on Etsy. It is

---

[3]"Put a little salsa in my pants and cha cha down the church aisles" is not a real saying that people use. I just made it up. But LET'S MAKE IT A REAL SAYING.

something we have heard pretty much for forever, right? But as you grow up, you realize it isn't always so simple. Sometimes dreams change. Or even with a solid goal and track to "success"—whatever you define that as—you find the road to glory is a heck of a lot harder to achieve than LeVar Burton made it seem on *Reading Rainbow*.

Or you may have no idea what those dreams are and find yourself floating aimlessly for a while. I heard a podcast episode where author Elizabeth Gilbert said she doesn't necessarily believe in all of us having one huge "life calling" that is a big secret we are supposed to uncover. She said sometimes believing that you are put on this earth for one specific purpose in regards to career or profession puts too much pressure on us. I think there is wisdom in that. Yes, some people may know what they want to do with their life and what lights them up like a neon retro motel sign, and that is awesome. But for others, discovering what they love and what fulfills them may come about more subtly and slowly, and that's okay too.

But just because something isn't simple doesn't mean you shouldn't fight for what is right and good anyway. What I think *isn't* okay is knowing in your gut and heart what you want to do but not doing it simply because you are afraid. Sometimes people are holding on so tightly to what they feel is safe, reliable, practical, that they miss out on the bigger plans meant for them all along. And that is a little mini tragedy that actually isn't all that mini. Because this life is so precious, and letting fear hold you back from fully experiencing that is just shortchanging yourself. Nobody else. Just yourself.

I truly believe if you clearly lay your desires before God, trust in his plan and his love for you, and don't let fear hold you back, you will end up where you are meant to be. But you know what? Even around that, in the messier moments where you don't know *what* you might want, let alone a path to get there, God is still with you, hearing you and guiding you, whether or not you know what direction that may be. Life is still good in those gray moments, and God is still guiding us through, wrapped in love.

Taking steps of faith, even when they feel scary, is a better option than taking no steps at all. Was I scared to move to Texas where I knew literally zero human beings, or even cows? Yes. But a fresh page had been laid out, and I was ready to fill it in with whatever that would evolve to be.

CHAPTER FOUR

GOD DIDN'T UNFOLLOW YOU ON SOCIAL MEDIA

Growing up I always thought it would be fun and romantic to move to a new state with my husband and start completely fresh, carving a new life out from scratch. Oh, little naive Katie and your overly optimistic brain. Bless your heart.[1] It turns out, starting over in a new city is hard. Really hard, actually.

Before we left Florida for our move to Texas, Kyle and I sold most all of our possessions we had collected in two short years of marriage and two tiny apartments. We had the most pathetic sale ever, on the sidewalk because of course when you are twenty-one you don't own a garage. You live in a garage, like we did. Someone bought a teapot from me, and I called it a success. Everything else we packed into our black Toyota Yaris in the most strategic way possible, doing things like shoving socks into glass cups and then wrapping them in a shirt to protect them from breaking on our drive across country.[2]

---

[1] Soon after moving to Texas, I learned that saying "bless your heart" is basically a polite way of saying "aww, look at you, you big dumb weirdo. I pity you" masked in a sweet-as-pecan-pie tone. Oh Texas, the land of big hair and big veiled insults.

[2] You are welcome for this unexpected pro packing tip.

We hugged our friends goodbye and set out to the great land of barbecue, blue skies, and boots, excited to dive right in to whatever God had for us. I had zero idea what the next year of life would look like, and that both excited and terrified me. Who we would meet, where I would work, if I would even like Austin. I hadn't been there yet, just had done a lot of Googling. Apparently Austinites liked to call themselves "weird" and eat a lot of tacos. Sounds like my kind of town.

As we rolled in to the city the next day, disorientated from being in a brand new place and having just driven eighteen hours, we pulled into a restaurant to put some sort of food into our bodies before we arrived at our apartment and began unpacking. I ordered a medium Diet Coke because caffeine is *life*. The lady brought me out a drink so big I could have fit my entire face right into the top of the cup and just lapped up my soda like some sort of deranged, Coke-loving cat.

"Oh! I just wanted a medium," I said.

"This is a medium."

Well. The rumors were true. Things really were bigger in Texas.

We moved into our apartment. It was a simple two-bedroom on the bottom level of a big complex. The floors were made of concrete and always cold, and there was a small balcony to sit on and try to get a bit of sun on your face under the big trees towering outside. There was a pool, and I could walk to both a Walmart and a Sprouts grocery store, so I felt I had everything and anything I would need to somehow survive. We worked on filling our space up with the few things we owned, and everything else we got from local thrift stores that lined Burnet Road, the main drag between our neighborhood and downtown. The most important item we got to fill our home with was cats. Two cats—Wilbur, who was named after a mountain in Glacier National Park, and Waffles, who was named after a real-life hippie Kyle worked with while in the musical *Hair*. Waffles the hippie had been hired to literally stand onstage naked, and, well, be a hippie. Oh, what a world we live in.

Kyle started his grad school program, meeting his new classmates he would spend countless hours with over the next few years. He would be on campus starting very early in the morning, and when he had rehearsals he wouldn't get home until after 9:00 p.m., so for most of the day I was alone, tasked with the exciting job of . . . finding a job.

I was optimistic, ready to hustle, and willing to do anything I could to carve out a new career path in writing for myself. But there was a small problem: it was 2009. And for all you young folks out there reading this, let Granny Katie tell you a tale. A harrowing tale of there being zero jobs available that year. The Great Recession had just hit, and unless I wanted to become a debt collector or uncertified renegade therapist for people struggling after losing their homes, the job options were very limited.

The year 2009 was one that felt like God unfollowed everyone on Facebook, took an extended all-inclusive vacation to the Bahamas, and left us to fend for ourselves in financial ruin. It was the worst year in recent history to quit your job, go somewhere you have zero connections, and try and start a new career with one measly year of work on your résumé. Yeehaw y'all. Hold on to your hats because we were about to get on a bucking bronco of struggle.

Every day I applied for jobs, all day long, which, for the record, is extremely *boring*. I spent hours filling out questionnaires and online application forms and making cold phone calls in a pathetic attempt to be extra proactive and "stand out," but all that made me do was stand out like a desperate dork. I tried to tweak my meager résumé to best appeal to whatever flavor-of-the-day job I was targeting. All for nothing. Zip, zilch, nada. Nobody was hiring. At least, nobody was hiring me.

We quickly blew through what small savings we had, and I realized I needed money, and fast, if we were going to be able to afford the essential basics of Austin life, which mostly consists of mass amounts of queso and breakfast tacos. And I guess also enough to pay rent and purchase some sort of food item not drenched in melted cheese.

So, even though I just spent the last year writing the news and online articles and actually making money with my journalism degree, I now had to resort to something I also unfortunately had experience in: waitressing. I just want to make it clear. I hate— HATE—waitressing. It just doesn't jibe with my personality. But also, I like making money, and waitressing is a quick way to do that. I did it all during college, so I had experience. I decided I would try to get a flexible waitressing gig while I continued working on freelance writing opportunities or looking for more steady jobs along that same line. So I put on my big girl pants, and I added my lovely food-serving experience to my résumé—yay—and walked into a local tavern that was hiring. It was dark in there, and there was a variety of sporting events blaring from the million flat screens hung from the ceiling. During my interview, they told me the restaurant was haunted, so that at least intrigued me some. I got the job, and I officially traded in my newsroom high heels for my Chuck Taylors and an apron and started serving burgers.

When you are a waiter, the one thing that really makes or breaks your experience is the guests you are serving. In Florida, it was Palm Beach socialites, which came with its own set of challenges, to put it nicely. At my new job, I decided to go to the polar opposite end of serving cranky, old, miserable-yet-insanely-rich people. This restaurant's main clientele was . . . frat boys. Young, loud, crude, football-loving, beer-slinging, skipping-out-on-checks frat boys. Basically, the general vibe of all my customers was your creepy Uncle Bob after one too many beers at a Super Bowl party, but a few years younger. It was brutal. I suddenly missed the old people who spit their caviar into a napkin and put it in your tuxedo jacket pocket like you were a living, breathing trash can. That seemed better than having to deal with a bunch of drunk bros screaming during the entire Longhorns game.[3]

But the job paid money, and I settled in. Since I was new, I was scheduled to work on Thanksgiving night, because that is exactly what people want after a day of stuffing your face with your family: to go out and stuff your face more. It turns out Thanksgiving was actually one of their busiest nights. All the frat boys would meet there after their family dinners to catch up with their old buds after being away at school for the past few months. That night, everything I hated about my job was amplified. The dudes were extra loud, extra crude. I got "Hey baby" a few times, and I would just stare at them blankly and make things really uncomfortable before walking away. One table walked out on their checks, which I got yelled at for by my boss. Because apparently in addition to being able to balance multiple plates of food at a time, I was supposed to also be psychic and know that the guy

---

[3]Okay, fine, I admit it. There actually was one fun part of the job. Everyone in the kitchen would congregate around the vat of queso in the back and just dip chips in and eat them casually throughout the entire shift. Yes, the same queso that we served to the customers. Hey—we didn't double dip at least! Looking back at this now I am beyond grossed out that we did that. But also, I miss that big tub of queso.

who said his friend was in the bathroom was lying and would slip out the door the second I turned my back. At another point, I was filling up sodas next to the very crowded bar when someone picked up my pitcher of iced tea, thinking it was beer, and if there is an unattended pitcher of beer, he of course had every right to snatch it up.

"Hey! Put that down," I said, trying to talk over the loud crowd surrounding us.

This bro, with his overpriced sports polo shirt—collar popped of course—and baggy cargo shorts, looked me in the eye for a second, surprised by me actually telling him *no*, and said, "Bitch." The tea splashed as he slammed it down, and he melted back into the crowd of other dudes. Well. Happy Thanksgiving to you too, Broseph.

That night I was driving home around 2:00 a.m. The bar closed at midnight, and we had two hours of damage control to deal with after that, sweeping up garbage and squished, cold food under tables, and wiping the stick of stale beer off of everything. Even though I had just worked my tail off, the tips were meager, and the amount of money I had in my pocket felt anything but worth it. As I drove home, I began sobbing, because that is what you do on a holiday when you are in a new city, away from your loved ones, alone, in a car and smelling like a Bud Lite burger smoothie. I was pretty sure at any moment a beluga whale was going to land on my windshield, thinking my crying was actually beluga whale mating sounds, as my guttural sobs sounded very similar.

Once I felt safe a whale wouldn't fall from the sky, I began yelling at God. I do think God welcomes our honesty and pain. And whale noises. Plus there wasn't anyone on the empty Austin road, so nobody could see me crying or talking out loud in an empty car, so I went all in.

I asked God why. Why were things not working out even remotely similar to how I thought they would be? Was this really where he wanted me? Waitressing in a job that just was *not* in line with my personality type, and barely making any money to boot? I felt I couldn't do this much longer. I cried to God that if this was it for now, to give me the strength. And to provide for us financially, because I didn't know how we were going to make it. I didn't know how I was going to keep showing up at that place that consistently beat my spirit down and barely covered our bills.

I felt so defeated. I had so many dreams and ambitions. I wanted to write and create and *work* doing what I loved and felt called to. Yet I was slinging burgers to pay for student loans on a degree I didn't even know if I would be using again.

Listen. If you are a waitress and enjoy it, I love that about you. I think that takes a special type of person. But it isn't me. This wasn't what I felt I was meant to be doing, yet it was the only door open for me, and it was driving me nuts.

When we left Florida and I decided to leave TV, I was fueled by all the optimism of a twenty-two-year-old fresh-out-of-college girl who was raised in the nineties hearing "You can do anything you put your mind to" about fourteen million times. I was *sure* I could find a cushy reporting job at some cute little magazine or website. Or I could write a book proposal in an hour one day, then get a publishing contract and begin churning out book after book.

Instead, God decided to give me yet another lesson in *waiting.* Everything in me wanted out of that restaurant and to start taking steps toward my long-term goals, but every single door was being slammed in my face, if I could find a door to begin with. I could barely find an air vent to crawl through.

But even in the wake of such rejection and defeat, I refused to give up. Perhaps that was the strength I begged for on the dark, empty Austin road that night. I kept going, kept trying. Because giving up is not something I am programmed to do.

When I wasn't getting a table of dudes another pitcher of beer and almost wiping out on the greasy floor in the process, I was back at our apartment keeping at it, applying, pitching articles, doing everything and anything and just waiting and hoping for something to finally come through. And praying all the while: God, I trust you, I am doing everything I can, but I am going to need you to make the next move because there is nothing more I can do with these two hands.

One day I saw there was a local writing conference coming up, and I decided to go. It was expensive and things were definitely tight financially, but Kyle was so encouraging, as he always is for stuff like this. As I filled out the registration form and entered in my credit card information, I was about to back out. I just felt it was too much of an extravagant expense, and I was nervous about making the investment. But then something wild happened. It was one of those small, private moments you know in your heart is from God. God doing something tangible before you, whispering a miracle right into your life in a subtle, sweet way.

This is the truth, guys. I was hovering over the X on the website to close out when a song came on my Pandora station. It was the song sung at my best friend's funeral—"Held" by Natalie Grant—and that stopped me in my tracks. The song had never popped into my feed before, and it never has again. For it to start playing at the exact moment I was about to cancel my registration meant something to me. I don't know exactly how or why everything works, but I do think it was a sign. So, I took the leap. Instead of the X, I hit submit.

As the conference approached, I was following their announcements on Twitter. Their social media team asked a question: "Tweet us why you are going to the conference, and you can win a consultation with a publicity pro." I gave it a shot and wrote arguably the single most important sentence of my life.

I said: "I am excited to meet other writers, because currently my only coworker is my obese cat Waffles."

Welp, apparently that did it. I won.

So a few weeks later, at the second day of the conference, at a tiny coffee shop table I sat down to meet with this publicity dude, Rusty. At the time, I didn't even really know what PR was, but hey, it was a free meeting and I am all about anything free. Right away I could tell Rusty was kind. He wore cowboy boots with his navy blazer and jeans, and had come completely prepared with a total website and social media consultation for me. He treated me with so much respect, like I was a high-paying client and not some weirdo with big dreams and a fat cat named after a naked hippie/delicious breakfast food. I, in turn, graced him with my jokes and dorky enthusiasm for books and writing, and we hit it off.

We were deep in a convo about books, platform building, writing, and social media when he paused, looked at me, and asked, "Do you want a job?"

I didn't know what exactly this job was, but I was pretty sure it wouldn't involve cleaning up cold, squished french fries off a bar floor at 2:00 a.m., so I quickly said yes. In retrospect, I should have played it cool and been like, "Oh, how interesting. Send me more details and I will think it over." But instead, knowing nothing about what it was or what it would entail, I just said yes. I will shred paper for you. I will do data entry until my eyes bleed. As long as I don't have to wear an apron and ask people, "Ranch or blue cheese?" ninety times a day, I will do it.

It turns out Rusty had just started his company a few months prior. He did publicity for authors and hired me on as a publicist. I was the fourth employee, and we all huddled around an IKEA table in a small office with no windows. And you know what? I loved it. It was the *perfect* job for me, combining journalism, books, and writing. And the thing is, I didn't even know that type of job *existed* until God straight up brought it to me on a silver platter via a man named Rusty. While I was waitressing for the previous year, Rusty was starting up his business. God had me wait, because what he wanted for me and what he knew would be best for me didn't even exist yet. Looking back, I would happily wait again for what ultimately turned out better than I could have ever designed on my own.

Sometimes you don't understand life's timelines or why things happened far differently than you expected. But for me, I feel if we trust God's plan, he will carry us through.

Learning that, and trying to fully lean on that, has gotten me through long, hard seasons of waiting. It certainly wasn't an easy road that year, but looking back, I can see how things worked together in the perfect timing. I do believe it is worth it to take risks and work hard, and work on strengthening your muscles of having hope and fighting for joy, even in the midst of crappy times. I think we can trust that what God has for us is the best option. And the strength you acquire as you fight to figure out what that is makes it all the sweeter.

CHAPTER FIVE

EMBRACE THE STUCK

ometimes in life, even though things seem to line up and be working out just fine, you know in your heart you are not where you want to be. It makes your soul itch but you don't even really know where to scratch. Do you scratch your leg? Your butt? There is no way to tell, but the itch is pretty dang present and annoying.

Confession time: in Austin, even after my hard year slinging burgers that ended in me finding a job that seemed perfect for me, I was still miserable. There—I said it! I know it makes me sound like a bit of a whiny blobfish who will never be happy, but the truth must be told at all costs.[1] This chapter just doesn't start out optimistic. The facts were that even though I tried with all my might to do all the things to be happy and enjoy our new city, I flat-out didn't like Texas and I wanted out.[2] But we were

---

[1] If you have never seen a blobfish before, please pause for a moment to google it. You're welcome.

[2] Apologies to everyone reading this from the Lone Star State, but I bet if you went to Minnesota in January you wouldn't exactly love it either. Sometimes it gets so cold your boogers ice over and your eyelids freeze shut. Everywhere is just not for everyone, and that's okay. I do commend you for your tacos however, and lovely weather. And amazing swimming holes. And fun cities. And access to the ocean. Okay, fine, maybe Texas is perfect. It's hard to say.

committed to a three-year graduate program, so I was stuck. And I don't like being stuck. As in, I hate it. I hate it so much.

On paper and social media Austin seems like a mecca of sunshine, tacos, gorgeous skylines, and happiness, all wrapped up in cute hipster, sustainable, locally sourced organic outfits. And it is! Among a lot of other great things. Austin is perfect! Just not perfect for me, which is the main difference, and our time there became one of the darkest periods of my life. Something about Texas just didn't click with my personality. And this was way before Enneagram tests were cool, so I was basically just in the wild west of trying to figure out why.

One of the greatest challenges for me was the people there were hard to connect with. People are everything to me. Deep, honest, real relationships bring me so much life. Especially ones that check all those boxes and then also make you laugh until you dry heave. But something about the way Texans operated made it hard for me to feel like I connected with many people on a genuine level. We did have our little crew and met some great friends eventually, but overall it just felt off in my heart.

Like most people who are born and raised in a particular region, Texans are thick with their own culture. Which is great and most times charming, y'all. They were their own country once—and they might be again! As they like to remind people . . . often.

People in Texas are just so ingrained in their ways and culture, which is fine and sometimes charming. But other times it felt like anything beyond their state's borders was essentially outer space. I would tell people I was from Minnesota, and they would look at me confused as they wondered just what part of Texas that town resided in. I would say it is up north, and they would be like, "Oh, like in Canada?" Sure. Why not. Close enough. I say this with the most love possible, but sometimes people are hard to connect with on a genuine level, and I think recognizing that and just looking for greener pastures is okay.

On the opposite end of this, any time I have ever met someone from New Jersey, we pretty much click instantly and dive straight into a mile-a-minute conversation as if we have known each other for years. I know that is a weird thing to say, but it's true! All I have to do is bring up Wawa, and they lose their minds and we instantly become lifelong friends. With Texas, it felt hard to *really* get to know people in the way my extroverted, oversharing heart really likes to. I tried! But they would look at me weird whenever I got too "much," too honest, too open, and then go and hide on their family ranch for the weekend.[3] The church we attended was as massive as the soda the woman gave me when we first arrived in Austin, and I felt lost and unable to form a community there. I volunteered, I joined groups, I made awkwardly forward conversations, but nothing was clicking. We were far from family, not really connecting with many friends, and Kyle would be gone from morning until late at night at school. I was lonely, bored, and ready to move on to the next chapter of our journey, but the page wasn't going to turn for quite some time.

And I don't say this just to dump on the Lone Star State and its lovely people. But what I want people to know is that it can be hard if a place doesn't feel like a great fit for you. On one hand, yes, we can always try to "bloom where we are planted." To work to cultivate relationships where we are at, even if it is hard. And you know what? God might surprise you and show you new ways

---

[3] I still don't understand what a "family ranch" is. I mean, do they have pet cows there? Are there tumbleweeds blowing in the wind as they cook beans over an open fire? I don't get it. A cabin, yes, I get. But everyone kept saying "ranch" all the time, and it just made me confused and want ranch dressing.

to connect and relate. But also, if you do everything you can to try and build community and feel "at home" but find doors keep being shut in your face, I think it's okay to ask God if you should move on and to help you to do so.

For me, I am such a fixer, possibly to a negative degree. If something isn't right in my life, I fix it. Or I make Kyle fix it. Gotta give the man the credit he deserves. But this season wasn't something I could fix or fast forward past. I had to keep walking right on through it until Kyle's school commitment was over. I was stuck, and stuck is just lame, and it was starting to wear me down.

Not one to give up a fight, I tried all the things that would normally make me "feel better." This always started with me going for a tiny half jog/mostly walk for twenty wheezy minutes. Endorphins, where art thou? Not in my brain, that's for sure. I started to do a lot of yoga. All the yoga. Five a.m. yoga. Hot yoga. Yoga classes that were essentially a structured nap. I googled mood-boosting herbs and took supplements. I would tell myself positive things and then get annoyed at having to say so many dang positive things to myself. Couldn't things just actually *be* positive without all the jabbering about it? All this peppy self-talk was exhausting. I would pray to God for help until my heart ached from praying. I drank delicious Texas margaritas and ate as much queso as my heart desired and just tried to "lighten up." You know, eat, drink, be merry—also known as the most hip Bible verse. But nothing was working. I couldn't get myself out of a funk, and this was one of the funkiest funks I had ever funked with. I felt awful, like my head was slipping under water and I was drowning, despite trying everything to not just stay afloat but get my feet on solid ground again.

Then, one warm spring day Kyle and I were driving down a winding South Austin neighborhood road, past cutesy vegan coffee shops and picturesque 1950s rambler homes. The sun was shining, the weather was perfect, Austin was as gorgeous as ever, and I was repulsed by all of it. At a stoplight Kyle glanced at his phone and saw an email that the job he was fairly sure he was going to get for the summer wasn't going to work out. His grad school stipend didn't pay during the off months, and it's pretty dang hard to get a job for such a short period of time. We had no other ideas or options besides that one thing we thought was a sure bet and were now left with a lot less income, a lot more stress, and zero ideas about how we would float through over the next few months. I didn't have one optimistic thought left in my brain. My inner cheerleader had officially overdosed on caffeine and passed out cold.

The stoplight turned green and suddenly, as Kyle kept driving, everything around us began to blur. The entire world seemed to spin and narrow, and it felt like seventeen elephants were sitting on my chest. I gasped for air as I begged Kyle to pull over, and with my face buried in my hands, I crumbled apart in the passenger seat of our tiny Toyota. There, on the side of the road in that adorable, sunshine-filled neighborhood, in one of the most fun, trendy cities in the United States, I had my first panic attack.

This was the final nail in the coffin that solidified what I already knew in my heart might be happening, but I had been denying and avoiding for as long as physically possible. I wasn't just moping or sad; my mental health was really struggling in a way it never had before. And despite all my best attempts to fix myself, I was just falling deeper into the darkness. I had never had a panic attack before, and at the time I felt embarrassed and ashamed—what kind of person completely falls apart like that? From the outside, everyone thinks I am this hyper, positive little ball of happiness. But what would they think if they saw me gasping for air feeling like I was about to internally combust, all over one little email?

Of course, it wasn't just the email. It was that my brain was out of balance, and my life was out of balance, and my soul was suffering because of it. I knew nothing I could do would be able to right-side up myself again, and reluctantly I decided I needed to see a doctor.

I was prescribed some mild antidepressants and began to take them, but it didn't come without a lot of inner debate and turmoil. Taking meds was new to me, and it felt weird to admit I needed that level of help. I asked God a lot of questions. I had to unpack a lot of stigmas that come with mental health that apparently I carried and were deep-seated in my brain. Things like why couldn't I just "choose happiness"? Didn't I see how blessed I was—why wasn't that enough? Why couldn't I fix myself? What did this all say about my faith in God? Did I not have enough faith for him to heal me?

All the inner dialogue and questions were negative. Not one comforting or empathetic thought passed through my brain. Would I ever cast those judgments against someone else? Never in a million years. But against myself? Apparently yes, and in a heartbeat. That is not okay, and I knew that. Still, it was hard to unlearn those toxic thoughts that were so ingrained in me.

But as I began to take the medicine, day by day, the fog would lift a little more, and with it, any shame and guilt over having to get that level of help. Because finally, after months of not even knowing how low I was, I felt like *myself* again. I didn't feel like some drugged-up, numb monkey who would never feel a genuine emotion again—like I feared I would on medicine—but the opposite. I felt like myself on my best day, something I hadn't felt in months. I could see things more rationally. I could see lights at the end of tunnels and appreciate the sunshine right there in front of me. I finally felt how I had wanted to feel and act but hadn't been able to get there on my own. On medicine, I felt whole again. Not extra, not less, but fully myself. Thank the Lord, truly. In that state, I could also see clearly how deeply I had been suffering. Sometimes you carry pain for so long you don't even realize its weight anymore. But when it was gone, I could finally stand upright again. And it felt amazing.

Over the next couple years, Kyle and I did the best we could as we finished out our time in the Lone Star State and planned for our life after grad school. He did amazingly in his program. When he acted on stage, the whole world seemed to be captivated by him. The gritty art that poured out of him while performing was one of the most beautiful things I have ever seen. Once, he played Mack the Knife—an old, macabre serial killer—and even I was creeped out by him. In that show he screamed an F-word so loud spit flew out of his mouth and landed on the audience members. Now that's acting, folks. Luckily this was pre-Covid. The best part was, his grandma flew in to see that performance. Enjoy the show, Grams? Your grandson is straight up horrifying and also spitting on people.

He also booked shows all over the country, and I happily tagged along, enjoying the new cities and cultures and mastering the art of living out of a hotel. We had a long stint in Seattle where I learned to appreciate cloudy days and hot bowls of pho. He did several shows in Dallas, and we fell in love with the buzz of that massive city and the actors in the company, who are some of our best friends to this day. Out of Austin, I felt I could breathe a bit better. And back in Austin, we fell into a comfortable stride, just doing our best while we had to.

I heard once it takes about two years to really feel established in a new city, and I found that to be very true. Things got easier after year two. We grew closer to people, and we had more of a life set up. And while we knew Austin wasn't going to be our forever home, we kept fighting to make the absolute best of it while we were there. We learned to love Texas Two Step dancing and would take long walks through our quiet neighborhood to the dingy, hole-in-the-wall restaurant for big plates of cheese fries or their homemade Twinkies on nights I felt too anxious to sit in our little apartment for one more stupid minute. We did the best we could and tried to enjoy each moment, even if my heart was still beating to move on, and quickly. But learning to slow down to the pace God sets for your life is sometimes the only option in front of you. So I tried my best to bend to that, instead of fighting against it, and to keep praying and looking forward to the next step that I knew would one day come.

Eventually Kyle graduated, and ahead of us was a long summer in a tiny town in our home state of Minnesota for a Shakespeare festival, and then a move to good ol' New York City where he had signed with an agent. My book-publicist and writing career would now be remote but in a city that was a mecca for all things publishing.

We were exiting this season, finally. The season that my brain and body and heart struggled with harder than any other in my life. But that is what it was—a season. And I can see now that in that time, though it felt like it lasted an eternity, my spirit was being carved and cultivated for the long haul. For future periods of waiting. Teaching me how to handle my mental health, which was now a part of my life. Teaching me about what I value in relationships, in a church, in a city. Teaching me God's plans are a lot bigger than what I can see with my two little eyeballs and to fully lean into that with peace.

Austin was my own master's program in learning how to not just "get through," but to actively pursue joy and happiness day by day, moment by moment, even when you don't want to. Not choose it, because it isn't that simple. But fight for it. And how to hold on to the hope that you know one day the light will come.

PART THREE

ADULTING REAL HARD, FOLKS

Hey there. A big part of "growing up" involves super disgusting things like figuring out how to pay taxes and buy health insurance. I can't tell you how much I loathe doing this crap. Gross. But alas, these obnoxious tasks keep coming at me! Stop ruining my vibe, IRS. But there are always going to be these little noncute hiccups of life that need to be taken care of. This part talks about some of these not-so-fun parts of getting older. Hopefully you can learn how to laugh a bit more at them, handle them with a little less stress and a lot more strength, and evolve into the full boss of a person you are as you karate chop the lame stuff into oblivion.

CHAPTER SIX

CELEBRATE TAX DAY (YEAH, YOU READ THAT RIGHT)

I saw a meme once that said, "Thank you American school system for teaching us how to square dance in fourth grade, but not how to pay taxes." Leave it to good ol' memes to speak such truth into our lives and make us laugh along the way. I am forever indebted to your wisdom and jokes, you little squares of joy.

But what that meme represents is a larger topic than just holding sweaty hands with a prepubescent boy as your gym teacher shouts out dance steps and your little Nikes squeak across the polished floor, and the IRS. The older you get, the more you realize there are a *lot* of things in life you are thrown into with an expectation that you should know how to do them but you don't. And the learning curve with those items can be brutal as you acclimate to what suddenly is expected of you now you are apparently a full-grown human being, even when you really don't feel like you are.

In recent years, this concept of "doing all the grown-up things" has been cutely dubbed "adulting." Thanks, millennial marketing companies for making everything such a trendy little quip. Albeit a cheesy term, *adulting* is a real thing. Going from cozy dorm dweller, where one of your biggest worries was if you were going to make it to the cafeteria before your favorite pizza ran out, to suddenly a full-blown adult who is expected to understand how to do gross stuff like navigate the American health insurance system without ripping every single strand of your hair out, can be tough. It is almost as if there should be a postcollege course called, well, "Life Postcollege 101." There you can learn very useful life skills such as living without ninety of your best friends down the hall from you, the art of faking it until you make it at your first job, and how to cook eggs without burning them into an impenetrable crust on the bottom of your pan every single time. Just me? Okay, cool.

Doing your taxes is one of the biggest, most obvious and brutal adult tasks that has to be mastered. Some things you can put off until you are a solid thirty-eight or so without anyone batting an eye at it, like retirement investing or wearing an appropriate length of jean shorts. But taxes cannot be put off, unless you want to just avoid them and surrender to your fate of living in a white-collar-crime minimum-security prison playing checkers with a fellow inmate named Funyon. Taxes need to be done, starting at the ripe old age of eighteen. Ouch! YOUR TIME HAS COME, YOUTH. You are now old. Whip out your W-2s and get calculating. Or math-ing. Or whatever boring number-related term you want to call it.

The longer Kyle and I were married, the more complicated our paying taxes situation became. No longer was it a "Here is my W-2. Here is the lump sum of money I made at my one single job. Done. Now where is my rebate?" Sigh. Those were the days. As we got older and deeper into our careers, we both had more regular day jobs and also a bunch of freelance writing and acting gigs. And then there were those pesky student loans. We both were also supposed to have LLCs as independent contractors, which blanketed everything else with a layer of extra confusion. There were papers with codes and lines and things I was pretty sure were just placed there to make my brain explode. It seemed as if Uncle Sam himself was on a personal mission to make me suffer every April 15. It was all one big confusing mess of . . . confusion.

The first year we really had a case of "hot mess taxes," we were in our apartment for about fourteen hours with papers strewn all about, typing things into TurboTax as if we knew what we were doing, but we certainly did *not*. A question would pop up on the software that could have been written in a foreign language, and Kyle and I would have to do straight up detective work to crack the code and figure out what the heck was happening. I had about three meltdowns, we both yelled, harsh words were exchanged, and tears were shed. Only from me. Kyle's tears are locked up in some sort of manliness fortress he has built around them. Somehow, we made it through to the end. (I think? Hard to say.) The stress had us so shell-shocked that by the end of the day we didn't really know exactly what we had just done but hoped it was something semiacceptable to the United States government. After we hit "submit" I fully expected the FBI to come and kick our apartment door down, screaming about how I was an imposter of an American who doesn't know how to correctly find the 3b box on my 1099 form, and immediately sweep me off to jail to meet Funyon. Get those checkers ready, Fun. I'm on my way.

The day after tax day that year, I immediately began fearing the next tax season. Yes, I know there are people you can hire to help with this stuff, but in your early twenties shelling out $400 for something like that is not an option.

The next year, when it was yet again time to hole up and try to decode this Nicolas Cage movie–worthy puzzle, it was no better than the year prior. For hours we sorted through documents, questioned the purpose of our existence, and cursed TurboTax and all the stupid questions it kept asking us. What is wrong with you, TurboBro? Have you no chill? Because what you are saying, I'm not understanding, and also, just stop. Kthx. It was as terrible as the year prior, and then, on April 16, I began to immediately dread having to do it again 364 days later.

But guess what. Tax day is coming, every single year. And I was sick of dreading it and stressing over it, time and time again. And I knew it was going to keep on coming back, like a stubborn wart, year after year, for the rest of my life.[1] And this is my life, and I insist on making it as beautiful as possible, even on stupid tax day.

So the next year I decided to fight back against the IRS. And I don't mean by not paying my taxes, doing some sort of strange solo protest outside of their headquarters in Washington, DC, or mailing in my forms with a whole bunch of glitter inside. Although that last option sounds a bit fun. I decided to fight back by doing everything in my power to make tax day fun. That's right—I said FUN. Well, at least mildly tolerable. I think that's an appropriate goal in this circumstance. But fun is better, if achievable.

So that next year, before our long, boring, terrible, gross day of taxes, Kyle and I stocked up on all the best stuff in life. We bought a lot of Diet Coke to be consumed during the process of completing taxes, and then champagne for after. We got snacks—all

---

[1] Ew, I said *wart*.

the snacks. A variety of chocolate-based products for my sweet-tooth dude, and chips and dip for me. We played French jazz music, because French music makes everything feel a bit more saucy. There is something that makes it a bit more bougie than plain ol' American jazz, and bougie is what you need on tax day. We lit candles, opened windows for fresh air, and made our tax day ambiance resemble that of a cute café we actually wanted to be at, not our apartment with unswept floors and a lot of confusing forms strewn about. We ordered pizza, because man cannot live on chips and chocolate alone. Also, like caffeine and snacks, pizza is a fast track to happiness. And, of course, we made tax jokes, because jokes help *any* situation that stinks but you have to walk through anyway.

That year, Kyle and I tried really hard not to fight with each other, knowing that scrounging for deductions is clearly one of our relationship triggers, and we were modestly successful. Was the day fun? No. Did we make it more manageable? We sure did, Sally.[2]

We did everything in our power to make this very terrible day a lot less terrible. And the next year, we did the same thing. We intentionally made space for beauty where there was previously none. With each year, we slowly began to understand all that is the madness of paying taxes and how to work together to make life a bit more enjoyable, even under times of stress.

But guess what? This method of making the ugly parts of life more beautiful doesn't have to be reserved for tax day. Any tough day or situation, with a bit of thought, can be intentionally made a bit more sparkly. And at the end of your life I don't think you will regret doing that.

---

[2]If your name is actually Sally, did this just freak you out?

Kyle is the master at doing this. For example, Tuesdays. I find Tuesdays to be one of the worst days of the week. Monday, we are all in it together, right? Oh Mondays, the worst, we all chuckle to each other as we post cute memes about it. On Wednesdays, you can see the light at the end of the tunnel. Friday, I can smell ya coming! But Tuesdays? What is the point! The weekend seems a year away, and nobody has a cute, funny meme or quip about how difficult a Tuesday can be. It just exists, like a filler day. It is the day I most often get a case of the postwork blahs. I just have to look at Kyle in a certain way, and he will be ordering pad thai, cuing up the latest thriller movie, and pouring us white wine spritzers while dancing around the kitchen to Frank Sinatra. Kyle knows, on some innate level, life is fleeting and short, and we always have the option to make it a bit more enjoyable, and I love that about him.

But it wasn't just Tuesdays and tax day when we did this together. There would be so many more adult things Kyle and I would have to figure out how to do together and not lose our minds in the process. Trying to buy our first house. Then, figuring out how to actually do a budget and stick to it so we could afford to buy the house. Shopping for health insurance because we were self-employed—disgusting. An atrocity. Then, after paying a million dollars a month for that health plan, having to navigate through the massive medical bills that come anyway. Fun. Or, discovering our house had a termite infestation. And maybe fleas once, but I don't want to talk about it. It is embarrassing and I blame Waffles. (The cat, not the naked hippie.)

The older we got, the more we realized if it isn't one thing, it's something else tricky that tries to sabotage our joy. That is just the nature of the beast, right? Clouds raining craziness keep on coming. But I am here to tell you that it's okay. No matter what is happening, we usually have the choice to play the French music, or worship music, or Lizzo—whatever the occasion calls for. Order the pizza.[3] Light the candles. Crack the jokes. Try with all your might to create beauty out of the mundane because the alternative of being squished by the dumb parts of life is not very fun.

Listen, I don't want to sound like a total Pollyanna. Fighting for beauty in the muck might not work perfectly. Some days are just not going to be that pretty, no matter what filter you put over them. But that's okay. My mom once said when I was having a bad day and complaining to her about it on the phone, "Oh well, you have a lot of good days too." And as blunt as it was, she was right. Yes, tax day comes, but so does Christmas morning. If you can figure out what works for you to make the hard days more palatable, you have won the game. I hope you fight for beauty and also expect it to show up. Even if it is only in small bits and pieces wrapped around one big ugly mess of a day. And that—the little bits of beauty that fit into the cracks around something hard—is definitely better than no beauty at all.

---

[3]Or sushi? Dang, now I want sushi.

CHAPTER SEVEN

SHUT THE CUPBOARDS, GIRL. BUT IF YOU FORGET, THAT'S OKAY TOO

Kyle and I once lived in a very creepy apartment. Those are always exciting, right? It was right after our first little garage place. The next year we "upgraded" a bit, if you could call moving from one old, odd apartment to a different old, odd apartment an upgrade. Our new place was at the top level of an old house now split into two units. It sat under the canopy of a large, ancient mango tree. I had never tasted a mango until I literally had them falling from the sky all around me. I feel like if a fruit falls by you, the least you can do is eat it. The mangoes would drop frequently, like little golden gifts from heaven. But then sometimes, it would drop in a more sinister way. Yes, I had sinister mangoes.

For example, one time a quick, feisty afternoon Florida storm was rolling in. I had just arrived home and was scrambling up our large outdoor staircase when a huge, green, unripe mango about the size and consistency of a softball fell from fifteen feet above me and hit me on the shoulder. If it had hit me on the head, I would have definitely been knocked out, in a thunderstorm, with more mangoes pummeling down on me. "Death by Tropical Fruit Mauling," the newspaper headline would say. But the other thing the mangoes did, which added to the creepiness factor of our old apartment, was fall from the tree onto our roof in the middle of the night and scare us awake. See? So sinister, that fruit. But delicious.

Also, in the apartment, the floors would creak constantly, even if nobody was walking on them. I woke up one night and clearly heard footsteps in the hallway, but I don't want to talk about it. It was just one of those old, odd places that made you feel a bit uneasy, especially if you were at home alone and it was dark out. And that is where I was one night, all by myself in the creaky, creepy, mango-shaded apartment with kitchen floors so rotten under the stained linoleum that my high heels would sometimes sink right into the ground and I would get stuck. That night, I was making microwave popcorn, and while it popped I went to grab my water cup from the living room. When I came back into the kitchen, every single cupboard and drawer was wide open. All. Of. Them. I gasped in horror—how did that happen? It looked like that terrifying scene from *The Sixth Sense* forever etched in my mind from my youth.

So there I was. Alone, in the dark, under a fruit tree that one time tried to kill me, and now apparently I had a ghost that did the classic ghost movie thing of opening every single cupboard. Why they do that, I am not sure. Perhaps ghosts are just trying to find the saltshaker.

But then, after a moment of confusion and fear, I realized it was not Casper trying to torment me. It was . . . me. I did it. I opened every single cupboard and drawer, didn't notice, and then moved onto the next thing, leaving them all wide open.

Here is the deal. I have a super-fast-moving brain that's always thinking ten steps ahead, usually to my detriment. I do things like leave cupboards and drawers open and have zero recollection of doing so. But it isn't just that—I will leave clothes piled in the middle of the floor in a heap the size of El Capitan, my bathroom counter is usually covered in various beauty products with missing caps, and I am really bad at getting toothpaste out of the tube without turning the top of it into a gigantic mint-flavored stalactite of old, dried fluoride-filled crust.[1] I am not the cleanest person. And truthfully, I don't like this quality about me. Am I allowed to say that? I know, self-love. But being messy brings me shame. Yet it keeps happening despite my best efforts at being a full-on Martha Stewart. Well, Martha pre–prison sentence and Snoop Dogg infatuation. Who knows what her home looks like nowadays.

But there comes a time when having shame about something gets old. I am sick of it. I am sick of having a negative inner dialogue about myself every time I try to find my keys and they apparently have been kidnapped by tiny house elves because they are nowhere to be found. Negative self-talk and shame get boring after a while. Negative self-talk is so 2010 of me, and I am ready to kick it to the curb like we did low-riding jeans and chunky highlights.

But being kinder to myself doesn't necessarily mean I let my life fall apart around me as I physically imitate the shoulder-shrugging emoji and leave a trail of trash wherever I go. Nope. It means I stop (note: at least I consistently try to stop) mentally

---

[1] Kyle has since resorted to getting his own tube of toothpaste because he just couldn't deal with how disgusting I was anymore. That is your daily dose of marriage advice for you. Making it work, folks, two separate toothpaste containers at a time.

beating myself up when I leave all the cupboards open. I give myself a bit more grace when I mess up. I throw that grace on like a comfy pair of oversize sweats, and it feels nice. And then, I fight extra hard to get better in this area where I clearly lack. I do this for myself and my mental health, yes. But also for my family, for Kyle, for the people around me. I don't want anyone to suffer because of my shortcomings. I try extra hard for them when doing it only for myself doesn't seem to do the trick.

I think that's part of becoming a real living breathing adult, right? Realizing where you are falling short, not making a big drama about it but simply making every effort to raise the bar in that area, for yourself and especially for the people you love. Then, when you fail—because you will fail every once in a while—learning how to correct yourself in love, not with an inner dialogue that sounds like your disappointed Great-Aunt Karen who lives with a lot of cats and thrives off of making others feel small and stupid. "Tsk—Katie, look how unorganized your cabinets are," she says as she strokes Muffy, her jerk one-eyed Persian cat that she for some reason brought along to look at my cabinets and ridicule me. That is what my inner mean voice sounds like—anybody else? Slow your roll, Aunt Karen. Also, you are not invited to Thanksgiving this year.

Remember the book *The Life-Changing Magic of Tidying Up*? If you haven't read it, I highly recommend it. I give it five out of five mismatched socks. That book was the stepping stone for me getting myself slightly better organized. Spoiler alert: the whole thing teaches you how to live with less and get rid of the junk in your life bogging you down. After I read it, as the author, Marie Kondo, gently guided us to do, I threw away about a million things. The most exciting part of that process is you "thank the item for its service" before you trash or donate it. Kyle and I love to talk to old, unused items like total weirdos before getting rid of them. It just makes cleaning more fun. "Thank you, outdated and chipped lamp we bought at Goodwill five years ago, for all the light you have given us. But you ugly, girl, and it's time to go."

That book also taught me the best method for folding shirts in the drawer so you can see everything inside all at once. I think of that trick often as I rifle through my drawer that is still just one big unfolded pile of T-shirts. But hey, at least it's *fewer* T-shirts, and at least I remember there is a better way. The book also teaches you how to roll pairs of socks together like sushi, and that makes me happy. Sushi socks. And with that, this may be a nice time to take a break and order a California roll with a side of spicy mayo.

Everything else in the book I mostly ignored, but it's still such a helpful catalyst to get my brain thinking about keeping things in line, and simplify my life in the process. And the simplification was the most important part. That is what I needed—less. Not more stuff and more to-do lists and more organizational items off of Amazon, but less. Less stuff weighing me down. Less choice. Just less. Simplicity. Her methods helped me form a very basic thought process about keeping things relatively organized, and from there I worked to evolve it to whatever was best for my family and my brain. It is still evolving, but at least now I have steps to take to improve.

But there was another book I read that did even more for me. It has an . . . interesting name, so brace yourself and don't judge me for it. It was called *You Mean I'm Not Lazy, Stupid or Crazy?! The Classic Self-Help Book for Adults with Attention Deficit Disorder.*

Okay, so listen. Back when I was prescribed antidepressants, one of the largest problems I was facing that brought me to the doctor besides panic attacks was an inability to focus on anything. ANYTHING. One day I was visiting my sister, Jenny, at her apartment in Los Angeles. We were working from home together. She was sitting calmly at her computer all day long, typing away, doing her work. I was up, in the kitchen, checking out the window, sending an email with two typos in it, fidgeting, checking the window again. There was such a noticeable difference between us, and I realized my lack of focus might be holding me back. And since I am an Enneagram Eight, I don't want *anything* holding me back. Move out of my way, people and brain fog.

When I discussed this with the doctor, he said the lack of focus was probably just a symptom of my depression, and I went with it because, you know, he was wearing a white coat and stuff. No formal screening or anything, and he just threw a prescription my way and that was it. And the medicine did help with being able to keep my attention on things, some. But I still have bad days when I can't focus to save my life. And I do things like leave the cupboards open and have zero recollection of doing it. I always felt my brain was wired a bit differently, and so when I saw this adult ADD book with the ridiculous name, I decided to read it.

Sometimes in life you pick up a book and it opens up a whole new world for you. That was this book for me. There in the pages I found myself. It was as if the authors were describing me exactly. I was half sure they had been spying on me through my iPhone camera all these years and wrote this book just for me and my issues. I could relate to pretty much everything they said. They said things I didn't even know were a symptom of ADD but were spot-on to what I experienced. And this freed something in me. This helped squash my inner Aunt Karen voice even more. I am not lazy, stupid, or crazy—I just probably have different wiring. But it didn't just illuminate that for me; it helped me get rid of the shame I felt about not feeling like I could ever completely keep my life together.

Yes, my toothpaste sometimes still is gross and never has a cap on it unless I remember to buy the kind where the cap is permanently attached—and I am seriously sorry about that, Kyle! Please accept this as my formal and last apology on the issue. But is that what I am really defined by? No. My toothpaste stalactite does not define me, and neither does yours, whatever that means for you. Your messy home or your slightly unhealthy obsession with having a perfect home—those don't define you. Your gross toothpaste or the way you meticulously roll it from the bottom up like it's an Olympic sport—those don't define you. These things we do, our quirks and hiccups, are just a small part of what makes us who we are and what we give back to the world. It's easy to put too much focus on them, fixating on the bad and ignoring the good, but it is important to fight against that with grace, strength, and a little bit of humor. Because jokes always help.

I know I will forever have to work really hard at getting better about picking up, shutting things, organizing things, and making a nice home for the other human beings who are forced to live with me. But I am okay with that, because hey—I'm trying. Heck, I'm even reading books with really awkward and embarrassing titles to try and improve. But when I mess up—it's okay. My worth isn't based on my ability to put a dirty dish immediately into a perfectly organized dishwasher.[2] We were made in the

---

[2]When I load the dishwasher, Kyle usually reloads it in a much more reasonable manner. He ends up getting like two times as many dishes in as I did, all nice and neat. Oh, so wine glasses don't just get casually strewn in horizontally across the middle lower section like I had them? Okay, good to know.

image of God, and as he tells us time and time again, his love for us is unconditional. Seems too good to be true, right? Well, it is, and it's worth thinking long and hard about that.

I am the type of person who is constantly trying to improve—it is just my nature. Even when it comes to laundry. But I do think the biggest thing I learned about being "clean" isn't how to fold my socks into a spicy tuna roll and throw away my junk, but how to throw away the shame I felt about not living up to some made-up, fueled-by-the-lies-of-Instagram set of rules I felt I needed to follow to be a good wife, mom, and fully valuable human being. Hey, I may not be able to notice an open cupboard, but I am really fun at a party. It's all about balance, right? And I am learning to be okay with that. I hope you are too.

CHAPTER EIGHT

GETTING HEALTHY
IS COOL, I GUESS

When you are in your early twenties, you can stay up until 3:00 a.m., eat a small bedtime snack of a dozen donuts, and then wake up the next day, run a 5k, and go about your afternoon like a normal, functioning human being. When you are in your late twenties, if you stay up until 3:00 a.m. eating a dozen donuts, you wake up dead. And they will have trouble fitting your coffin shut because you ate twelve donuts on your last day on earth and you grew to the size of Hagrid in Harry Potter instantly because of it.

When you are young, you have the metabolism and energy of a goat who has had one too many triple pumpkin lattes. You can eat an entire gaggle of everything-flavored bagels with veggie cream cheese in a weekend and lose four pounds by Monday just by sneezing once. But when you get older it doesn't happen like that anymore. You put one extra sprinkle of everything bagel seasoning on your egg white scramble and you gain twelve pounds instantly. Do you feel me on this? It is just one of those harsh, "growing up" things you can't avoid or conquer without a little introspection and work. Which, ugh.

After Kyle and I got married we started eating full, adult-human-being-sized meals together every night, then falling into a lovely routine of eating buffalo dip packed with multiple forms of dairy products in it, all washed down with a side of Miller High Life while watching ghost hunting shows until midnight. Because of this, my body started getting lumps and bumps in areas that I wasn't really loving. Listen up, you. I am *all* about body positivity and feeling good in your skin no matter what size or shape you are. But I wasn't feeling good in mine, and for good reason. I ate more bowls of dip a week than hours spent exercising. So the math is clear. I wasn't doing what was best for my body.[1] I needed to work out.

But I had a big problem. I hated exercising. The elliptical was like a thirty-minute jaunt into a boring realm of hell, and hand weights just reminded me of tacos, and I had no idea what to do with them, nor did I care to really find out. I read once you should find an exercise you enjoy if you want to stick with it, and the basic "work out like a beef bro" gym certainly was not doing that for me. I knew I needed to look elsewhere to find something I actually wanted to do so I wouldn't quit on it faster than I could heat up another bowl of cheese in the microwave.

In high school I was obsessed with dance. I was at the studio five days a week, year round, for hours at a time, and I didn't think of it as exercise really, even though I was working my butt off—literally and figuratively. I simply loved every minute of it. There was nowhere else I would rather be than at the ballet barre—a real ballet barre, not some Pilates torture session with way too many women in Lululemon pants I couldn't afford. So, it makes

---

[1]But also I love dip so much.

sense that swapping satin pointe shoes and fake eyelashes for sneakers and a stinky gym just doesn't get me excited. Logic would then tell me dance class would be a natural first place to start. I found an adult ballet class, dusted off an old leotard, shoved my body into it as best as possible, and headed in to give it a shot.

Being at the barre and plie-ing my way through the class brought back a few nostalgic memories, but it was overwhelmingly a very mirrored reminder of how far I have drifted from high school physically. Exercise is supposed to be about endorphins, not staring at your jiggly tights-covered thighs and having flashbacks of your cranky ballet teacher screaming at you about how you need to suck in your gut. SUCK IN YOUR GUT. Well, lady, things just don't suck in like they used to anymore. I loved my childhood filled with dance class, but I was also very okay with letting that go for something a bit more friendly.

So my exercise quest continued. One day, while I was googling gym memberships and eating an insane number of tortilla chips—organic, so that makes them a health food—I came across a description of Zumba and thought I would give it a try, as it is basically dance with just a little more booty shaking for cardio purposes. Or so I thought. I went to my first class only to realize it is a LOT more booty shaking, with a hefty side of twerking and a few butterfly pops thrown in for good measure. As a white girl who grew up lighting liturgical candles at my Lutheran church in Suburbia, Minnesota, booty shaking makes me uncomfortable. It's just how I was raised. I had coworkers who made it a point to say "happy hump day" to me every Wednesday, just to watch me squirm and yell far louder than was office appropriate, "GROSS." So in my first Zumba class, when the instructor had us put our hands on the ground and shake our butts in the air as fast as we could like Miley Cyrus in her best and worst moments, I melted into a puddle of awkwardness. I glanced around to see if anybody else was as embarrassed as I was, and it didn't appear that way, so I decided to just go for it, putting inhibitions behind me all for the sake of exercise.

In fact, in that Zumba class there was one attendee who seemed to be thoroughly enjoying himself, more so than most. Among a sea of sweaty, booty-shaking women stood a middle-aged man with an intense comb over and huge 1980s creepster glasses, wearing a dingy white T-shirt, knee-high white tube socks, dad sneakers before dad sneakers were cool, and a permanent smile on his face. I know my description makes him sound like the subject of the next Netflix serial killer documentary, but he truly seemed harmless and genuinely there to get his workout on, not caring that he stood out from the rest of the crowd. This man apparently loved Zumba—a lot—as his sweat-soaked shirt attested. He was laser focused on the teacher and her every move, and he enthusiastically followed along. But his moves, bless him, resembled nothing like what the teacher was doing. She would do an arm roll to the right, he would shuffle along and flail his limbs about like a spider in a toilet bowl trying to survive. She would shake her hips to the left, he would aggressively move his hips in an erratic pattern that resembled a drunk electric eel. He genuinely tried to mimic the teacher but then ended up doing his own creative free form of a movement, sprinkled with a few claps every now and then because, I mean, who doesn't love a random clap? CLAP. See? Kinda fun.

I couldn't help but glance at him sporadically, though I am sure staring at each other's dance moves was crossing some line of Zumba etiquette. I found him amazing, horrifying, and very, very entertaining. You go, middle-aged Zumba man, you go. The point is, he had found his exercise stride. He was doing it *right*—getting his sweat on and loving every second of it. The next few times I went to class, he was right there in the front, doing his avant-garde shimmy and shake, bless him. But for me, after a few classes, the excitement of Zumba wore off. I just didn't have the passion that the stained-shirt-tube-sock-wearing older man did. Plus, there is only so much hip thrusting in public one can logically take without feeling weird about it. So I set out to find something else.

I decided perhaps yoga might do the trick. I had taken a few classes in the past and enjoyed it. My first yoga instructor once had us close our eyes in a shavasana and smoothly talked us through a few minutes of relaxation. When we opened our eyes, he had completely changed his outfit. So . . . that was interesting. My next yoga teacher at a different gym was a tiny, seventy-five-year-old woman who reminded us of that fact every few minutes. "I'm seventy-five!" she would scream, then lift up her shirt and slap her six-pack abs. After class we would line up, and she would douse us with essential oils, either orange or lavender, and it was lovely. And this was before essential oils were so *trendy*. I loved that crazy old fit lady, but we eventually did one of our cross-country moves, so I could no longer gaze at her glorious abs while she dripped oil on my wrists. So far with yoga, I liked the quirky teachers, the no-pressure atmosphere, and the relaxed way I felt after a class, so I figured it was the place for me and was hoping it would be the thing that would keep me sticking to a workout routine happily.

After our move, I did a little googling and saw that a studio had recently opened close to our house and they offered a free week for new customers, so I decided to check it out. My first time there, I walked into the dimly lit room, unrolled my mat, and tried to get into my zen state, whatever that actually means. There was just me and one other man in the room, who was in the front with his legs crossed, and he was sitting stoically forward. I caught a glimpse of his face in the mirror and inwardly gasped. It appeared I was about to practice yoga with John Lennon's ghost. He was identical to a 1969 version of the Beatle, complete with little round glasses, squinty eyes, and long, straggly brown hair. He caught me glancing at him in the mirror and immediately went from meditative, quiet yogi to the chattiest of all yoga room chatters, breaking the cardinal rule of never talking in the studio unless one of your limbs falls off and you need to alert the authorities.

He began rambling, "Have you been here before this place is totally rad I really dig it it is actually my second class today well at this studio at least I was here this morning but then went to another studio and now I am back so I guess that makes three yoga classes," forming one long beast of a sentence. I politely nodded and tried to answer him, but he kept going. "Also I am so stoned right now. So. Stoned," he said before turning back around, crossing his legs, and staring at the mirror in a trancelike state again. Well then. Eventually, other (sober) yoga practitioners entered and the class began, and except for a few random bouts of interpretive dance off his mat (seriously, he did this; he and the Zumba creepster would have been good friends), John Lennon behaved. And I was hooked. On yoga, not John Lennon's dance moves. The yoga class kept my attention and was the perfect amount of working out without feeling like my lungs were going to explode, and I left feeling energized, happy, and ready to return.

After that class, I never saw the drugged-up yogi again. I assume his free week at the studio ran out and he moved on to greener pastures. Pun intended? Possibly. Despite this oddity, I fell completely in love with the yoga studio and signed up for a monthly membership. I actually *liked* going, so much so that I began attending the 5:45 a.m. class almost every day. The euphoric, tranquil feeling I had after class became addictive, and I could tell I was getting stronger. Soon I was able to do a headstand, which in itself is a small fitness miracle.

But you know what? The best part of yoga wasn't just the workout but the beautiful, diverse people who were right there practicing with me. From the large older man with the insanely long and tangled back hair to the tiny, fit college student with a perfect tan, each was uniquely beautiful and powerful no matter what level of athleticism they were at. There was such an overwhelming sense of acceptance and encouragement in those classes. Nobody was yelling at me to suck in my stomach or watching me try to hip-hop dance to a Beyoncé remix. Whatever shape, size, or amount of back hair we had, in yoga we were working together toward the common goal of our own sense of fitness, peace, and strength. Even though I didn't have the ballet body I did when I was seventeen, I was working toward a better version of myself, and that is what really mattered. And I think that is all that matters with whatever form of exercise you choose to do. With yoga, I began to accept where I was physically and felt great that I was moving forward. The end. And in the process, I actually liked exercising—a small miracle in itself.

Life is so quick, juicy, and sweet, and there isn't enough space in mine for feeling bad about my body or for not being at a place I was when I was younger. What there is room for is doing exercise that I enjoy, because it is good for my brain and my health, and it makes me feel like a million bucks. That is all I can focus on in this phase of my life—no Beachbody six-pack and thigh gap for me, sorry all you people lurking on Facebook looking for new team members. Whatever it is you love to do physically, I hope you can make the time to find a space where you feel the best about yourself—about how you feel and, yes, even how you look. Life is short. You are worth it.

But also, I really do think John Lennon is still alive somewhere, doing a lot of yoga and drugs and probably watching Netflix with Elvis on the weekends. I hope they invite the Zumba creepster as well.

PART FOUR

CONTENTMENT AND PEACE

Hey there. We all have a past, right? There comes a time when we all need to accept where we came from, make peace with it, and move forward so we can live more fully. That is what this part is about. Learning to let go of what was and fighting for what you *want* is a huge part of growing up. Finding contentment. Because it is possible, you just have to work for it a bit. God can heal, and God can mend, and God has things he wants for you that are better than what we could ever plan for ourselves. I hope you can let go of any junk holding you back and move forward into a place of strength and joy. Because being weighed down is LAME and I am over it.

CHAPTER NINE

MAKING PEACE WITH YOUR ROOTS. HOMETOWN ROOTS, NOT HAIR ROOTS[1]

Some people who grow up in the Midwest want to leave it the moment they graduate high school. The reason may be as simple as wanting to live in a place where their eyelashes don't freeze shut in the winter when they are scraping the ice off their windshield in the morning. That is the camp I was in. Shortly after I threw my tasseled hat in the air, I went straight to Florida and headed immediately to the beach to catch up on all the vitamin D I had been deprived of over the past eighteen years.

But then there is the other side of the spectrum—the people who grew up in the Midwest, love it, and will never leave. Sometimes, they don't even want to move out of their hometown. They love ice-fishing all day in the winter and then the feeling of their butt cheeks stinging as they thaw out by the fire inside in the evening. They like going to the lake in the summer and cooking a variety of casseroles that all contain a can of cream of something

---

[1]Actually, hair roots are fine also. Hair care is expensive and time consuming. Let those roots fly free if you want. You do you.

soup. They love the way the cornfields wave when a strong summer storm is about to hit and have built up a solid immunity to the bite of a mosquito. They wear their thick accents proudly and own multiple shades of flannel shirts. And you know what? I respect all that. Especially the casserole part.

The third group is people who grew up somewhere they didn't necessarily love, never left, but are still wondering to this day, *What if I had? What if I had the courage to take that leap, make the move, take the risk? What if I had moved to Los Angeles to chase my dream of becoming a sea monkey trainer/magician/leotard-wearing opera singer like I had always dreamed of? Oh well, I will never know now. Please pass the tater tot hotdish, I need to eat my feelings.*

Where we grow up or come from in life can be great, boring, or even painful. As an adult you are given this chance to decide where you want your future to play out, and that is no easy decision to make. As we get older we have the chance to reflect a bit more on where we came from that *wasn't* our choice; rather, it was where we were born, raised, and required to live. We can decide if that was good for our souls, or not, and then act accordingly.

But even then it can get murky. We may be somewhere we love but still yearn for home. Or be home and wish with everything in us we were elsewhere, but it just isn't in the cards at the moment. For me, I left the Midwest and it was a solid ten years until I began to realize how much I actually missed it. And loved it. I can look back and see that while I was ready to hightail it out of there as soon as I could, there was also a lot about it that shaped who I was and that I could embrace. I now love and proudly wear my flannel shirts and fur-lined hats and say "uff da" as much as I can whenever I go back. It took me leaving my home for a long time to really learn to appreciate it, and I know I am not alone in that.

As the list of new states Kyle and I moved to grew, I began thinking more and more about where we *came from*. As we learned the new ways communities and cultures operated, I couldn't help but look back and reflect on my own culture. And, to be honest, I felt like I didn't have any. That bothered me. I mean, genetically I am a mix of Norwegian, English, German, and Neanderthal. Seriously. My mom took a genetic test, and she has more Neanderthal DNA in her than 84 percent of the population, which is my favorite fact about her. And honestly that may be the part of my DNA I most identify with. I am loud, I like being outside, and sometimes I am a bit aggressive. But I am not about to start a family tradition of wearing woolly mammoth onesies and grunting around a fire while eating leaves. No fun in that.

See, I was born and raised in a town named after raccoons. Coon Rapids, to be exact. True story. So embarrassing. The city is somewhat infamous in the Minneapolis area due to the Podunk and frankly racist name. There have been a few campaigns to change the name for that reason alone, and I fully support it. When I tell fellow Minnesotans that is where I am from, I get a "look." Half pity, half disgust, as they have heard the jokes Minnesota radio stations spew out about Coon Rapids, as if it were the underbelly of the Midwest. When I tell people *not* from Minnesota the name of my hometown, I usually get a gasp, a half laugh because they think I am joking, then a look like "waittt . . . really?" I love slapping on my thickest Minnesota accent when I tell them about it. I am sure they instantly envision me growing up in some backwoods, rundown barn-cabin hybrid nestled under a lot of pine trees where we bred raccoons for stew meat. But Coon Rapids definitely isn't that. That would maybe even be an improvement—at least there is some excitement in that scenario. Coon Rapids is simply a Midwestern suburb. You know the type—each 1980s boxy home looking identical to the one across the street, all centered around sprawling, concrete-laden shopping centers with such cultural luxuries like Costco and Old Navy.[2]

Growing up, I couldn't wait until the day when I could leave the Midwest behind for greener pastures. Actually, for a place where pastures didn't exist altogether. I wanted that taste of salty ocean air the moment I walked out of my apartment in the morning. Or, even better, a tangerine sunrise over the Manhattan skyline or the faint outline of mountains against a sky overflowing with stars. Basically, anything, anywhere seemed better than a town where the best thing to do on a Saturday night was head to TGI Fridays for 99-cent breadsticks—you get six to an order, FYI. Trust me, I ordered that just about every weekend in high school with my friends. Such a bargain. I'm sure the waiter hated me, but it's not my fault they have such a filling yet cheap item on their menu!

I felt like to be the true, full version of myself, I had to live in a city high-rise and wear all black and sunglasses covering at least half my face, but possibly even more. Basically, I always envisioned the best version of myself as resembling Moira from *Schitt's Creek*.[3]

Growing up in the slow, calm Midwest, my spirit felt restless, like I didn't quite belong where I was. I wanted adventure. I wanted art and culture and new experiences. I wanted to be out of my little bedroom in my parents' basement and in a place of my own, one that wasn't decorated with a deer head mounted on

---

[2] I do love me an Old Navy, though. Their Rockstar jeans and $3.99 black flip-flops have been a fashion staple of mine for a long time. #sponsoredad #justkidding

[3] I do still want to be her in a lot of ways. Except for the wigs. Wigs are itchy. I don't have that level of beauty commitment.

the wall.[4] I wanted to find where I felt I fit in, because Coon Rapids wasn't it. And I think that's okay. We are all not going to be born into the perfect city, state, community for us. Would it be easy if we were? Yes! Of course it's amazing to love and thrive exactly where you were planted from day one. That is a gift, truly. But it's okay to explore other places that may be a better fit. What isn't okay is to ignore what you truly feel God calling you to out of fear or the desire for comfort. Accepting blah mediocrity while ignoring tugs at your heart to truly find where you are meant to be is a fast track to crushing your soul.

When we moved to Texas, the itch I felt about not having my own sense of culture began to really bother me. Texas is overflowing with traditions, fresh local foods, and statewide pride. When people think of Texas, they know what it's all about: boots, tacos, and wide blue skies. And for the most part, they're right. But when outsiders think of Minnesota, what comes to mind? Snow? Weird accents from the movie *Fargo*, which isn't even based in Minnesota? Was that all we had to offer?

The city of Austin might be the most polar opposite town from Coon Rapids. While my hometown thrives on familiarity, chain restaurants, and normalcy, Austinites proudly wear T-shirts that say "Keep Austin Weird" and would rather sit on a cactus than be caught walking into a Chili's. Coon Rapids folk love Chili's—so exotic. Austin has a local Tex-Mex joint or a BBQ place on every corner. In between those are independently owned coffee shops, breweries, or vegan restaurants. BBQ and vegan—the range in Austin swings wide. In Minnesota, our range swings between Target and Walmart.

---

[4] I have been waging a twenty-year campaign for my dad to take the freaking deer head off the wall in our family room and at least bring it to our cabin where deer heads on the wall are more socially acceptable. He refuses. Please sign my "remove my dad's deer head from the wall" petition on Change.org.

But in the same way leaving where you are from can teach you so much about who you are, sometimes going back can do the same, and give you greater clarity about who you are meant to be moving forward. There is value in embracing where you came from, even if you have to really hunt for the good parts about it. And sometimes God takes you somewhere that on paper you wouldn't ever think would be the best fit for you, but guess what? God knows better than what our little pea brains can comprehend, and you end up falling in love with the place and learning more about yourself in the process.

Our last year in Austin, God decided to give me a crash course in my Minnesota culture and roots in the most unusual but sweet way. The first lesson was taught to me in a very unexpected place—downtown Seattle. Kyle and I were staying in the beautiful, gray, rainy beast of a city for a few weeks while he did a play at Seattle Children's Theatre. We were living in a hotel in the Queen Anne neighborhood that gave out free packets of Starbucks to brew in your room, and it only took a few minutes to walk to the Space Needle. It was amazing.

Two of our oldest friends from Minnesota happened to be living in Seattle at the time. One night they told us they had a surprise. We walked down a quaint street with old buildings, dark alleyways, and bouts of street art, and came to a place called Zayda Buddy's Pizza & Bar. I walked in, and it was like I had walked into the exact dingy bar tucked away in the woods near my cabin. The Minnesota Wild were playing on every TV screen. There were neon Grain Belt Beer signs all over the walls and a loon painted on the bathroom door.

Just before my trip to Seattle, I was telling my coworkers about my recently acquired skill of making a loon call by blowing air through my intricately placed thumbs—something my father has been doing for my entire life at our cabin and I could never quite master until the ripe age of twenty-six. On warm, buggy summer nights, he sits on the back porch of our cabin and makes the call, and the loons answer him back from across the lake. It is awesome. I was showing my coworkers how I can now, after a quarter century of trying, make the call as well. They all blankly stared at me until one of them asked, "What the heck is a loon?" I didn't even try to explain. My heart was broken. What alien planet was I living on?

So when I saw that little loon painted on the door, I nearly cried from happiness. My friends had surprised us by taking us to a Minnesota-themed bar in the middle of downtown Seattle. It made no sense, but I was in love.

When I opened the menu, I couldn't believe how Minnesota accurate it was. They had every single food item I ate growing up, down to tuna casserole with a side of Pringles. I was fairly certain they consulted my mom before opening this restaurant. We ate so many Pringles growing up my mom once peed in an empty can of them on our boat when it was too cold to go in the water and she didn't want to disrupt our fishing trip.[5]

It was as if they had stolen a copy of my mom's shopping list circa 1997 and shared it with all of Seattle. Except it wasn't just unique to my family, I realized. It was Minnesota food. This is what I was raised on, this is what our state eats. While I thought it was nothing but bland, Middle-America, basic potato- and cheese-based items, it is in fact unique to our region. Sure, it doesn't come with a flashy song and dance like a sizzling plate of

---

[5] I will never get over this.

fajitas does, but it does come with warmth, love, and an easy ability to tote it to the local Lutheran church potluck.

That trip to the Minnesota bar made me realize that what I thought was just lame-o Midwestern nothingness was actually kinda quirky and fun. And their menu gave the option to add Velveeta to any dish, so . . . God bless the Midwest for that.

Shortly after our trip, Kyle finished grad school in Texas and signed with an acting agent in New York City. It looked like my Moira Rose dreams were actually about to come to fruition. But before we made our big city move, he had signed on to do a summer-long Shakespeare festival in southern Minnesota. Instead of being twenty minutes from Minneapolis, this little riverside city of Winona was two-and-a-half hours away, down winding roads through tree-covered bluffs. I honestly didn't even know Minnesota had bluffs! Where our cabin is up north, we have pine trees and lakes. The end.

We moved into an oddly nice and spacious dorm room at Winona State University, which hosted the festival every year. We were a few blocks from the Mississippi River front and a couple blocks from their small brick storefront downtown main street. And we were right next to the local VFW, which apparently was the *place to be*. Almost every night after rehearsal, I would join Kyle and his cast there. We ate the free popcorn from the popcorn machine, drank $2 whiskeys, danced to polka music on polka night, and participated in their meat raffles. We were surrounded not by strip malls but rivers and lakes that we fished on our lunch breaks. And we met the friendliest people who truly were living up to the "Minnesota nice" idiom. I began to happily join them. My summer uniform became cut-off jean shorts, a camo button-up, and rain boots. I leaned in hard to the Midwest ways and loved it.

This tiny Mississippi River town was just what I needed to see that, while yes, I may have grown up going to TGI Fridays a lot, there was more to where I came from than that. I just needed a few years of living somewhere else before coming back to home base with a fresh perspective and a whole new appreciation for the art of wearing fleece-lined flannel shirts and insulated jeans. And while yes, I do love living in big cities and by the ocean, and basically anywhere it doesn't snow nine months out of the year, I also really love slow afternoons fishing on my family's lake. I love that I know how to bait a hook and take fish off the line after catching them. I love walking through the woods wearing an extremely manly outfit and a hat that has a mosquito net hanging off it. I love that my mom can call me because she ran into an all-female Bigfoot hunting club called the She-Squatchers up by our cabin and my first thought is, *How do I join?* I love that I don't need to wear a coat unless it's under ten degrees, and I know how to de-ice a windshield. I have learned to love where I came from and also love the side of me that wants to be somewhere else.

Pasts and childhoods can be very painful for some, or they can feel idyllic and like you want to run back and hide in the nostalgia. There are a lot of people who land between both of those extremes. Either way, perhaps what is most important is coming to a point where you simply reflect on where you came from and learn from it. Take stock of what worked for you and what definitely didn't, and then move forward from that space. Carve out your own adult life around that reflection in a way that fits who you are today. Not who you were, but who you are now. And, of course, who you want to become in the future.

CHAPTER TEN

GO BUY A WHITE PLATE AT THE DOLLAR STORE

*L*iving in a dorm room that summer in Winona, we only brought with us the very, very basics required to live. We had recently (yet again) sold most everything we owned for our big move to a postage-stamp-sized apartment in New York City, so we didn't own much anymore anyway, and packing even lighter came easy this time around. That summer, we lived out of one suitcase of clothes and just a few things for our kitchen. That was it.

I have learned to love our times of living with nothing more than the basics. Yes, you may end up wearing the same pair of jeans thirty-five days in a row, but I do that at home anyway when I have a full closet of clothes to choose from, so whatever.

Simplicity really does open up your life to so much more joy. We don't need stuff. Sometimes we actually need less stuff so we have more room to expand our lungs and take big, full breaths. But even more important than having less is learning to fixate on less. Because sometimes we don't have a lot, but we *want* a lot, and that can be a dangerous place to be. Sometimes we have way more than we need, yet we are still addicted to trying to get more.

Bigger, shinier, prettier things and homes and vacations and wardrobes and whatever other stuff to subtly photograph on Instagram and low-key make others jealous.

I feel best when I am filled up on God, community, creativity, and love. Those are the things that make me feel most alive. An Apple watch does not. But this is not some radical call for you to sell everything and go join a commune in the woods.[1] Having a home, a job, and some food every now and again is important. But having less can sometimes make you feel like you have more. At the very least, it's worth exploring the option of simplifying your life and stuff, and evaluating how you view possessions. Plus, having less laundry to do is always a bonus.

But when you are about to enter a season of living with less, whether intentionally or not, I hope you remember one thing: don't forget to get a white plate from the dollar store.

The little dorm that summer in Winona wasn't the first time Kyle and I had lived simply. During grad school, there were several times when we left Austin for a few weeks of hotel life in different cities and states so he could act in a play. Looking back, these simple times when we lived out of a suitcase and had a few possessions with us were some of our sweetest days. We didn't have a lot of stuff, but what we lacked in possessions we were overflowing in the stuff you can't add to your Target drive-up order. Mostly that meant wonderful people around us. We usually made fast friends with the other actors, and there were plenty of cast parties, which are my favorite thing ever—says the lady who has never once acted in a play before yet has been a dorky plus-one to countless celebratory postproduction events.

---

[1] It honestly does sound tempting, though. Anyone want to get this started?

It is just a fact of life that actors throw the best parties, and also, there are always snacks there, so . . . ya know. Snacks. Fun dramatic people. Drinks. Cast parties are simply the best of the best and an extrovert's dream.

Also, during these times away, we were gullet-deep in creativity and actively pursuing our passions and what charged up our souls, like Lizzo on her best booty-shaking day. We were doing our art, and there is something magical about being in a routine where that is a regular part of your everyday, because it is very easy to fall out of that. During shows Kyle was usually buzzing with this unique brand of happiness, filled up on the energy he got by memorizing lines, performing, and figuring out his character. I loved seeing him so full on all of that. And while he was at rehearsal or performing every night, I was at a coffee shop, working on my writing and taking regular steps toward my own goals, and it felt amazing.

In the normal humdrum of life, it's easy to get distracted—or purposely distract yourself—in a routine of work, Netflix, sleep, repeat. It is often easier to avoid doing the hard stuff, the scary stuff, the stuff out of your ordinary. But whenever we were separated from our typical routine and forced to carve out a simple, new way of living our day to day, we somehow made more space for the good, juicy things of life.[2] When we were away for shows and given a blank slate, he was acting, I was writing, and we were exploring new cities, our hearts felt full— to use that cheesy, cringeworthy yet true statement. Slap it on a coffee mug. Heart is full.

But back to the white plate at the dollar store.

---

[2]*Juicy* is a gross word.

Before our very first extended hotel stay, I went to Dollar Tree—one of my shamefully favorite places to throw my money at—and bought a few things to take with us. Some simple silverware, two plastic glasses, and these two ceramic white plates that kind of had high edges around them, so they could double as a bowl if needed. A plate-bowl combo. A plowl, if you will.[3] They were perfect. They didn't get insanely hot in the microwave and burn the flesh off our hands like most dollar plates did. They were sturdy and didn't break when we carted them all over the country in a suitcase shoved next to our underwear stash. They were deep enough to hold our microwave mac and cheese ... I mean our fresh salads ... that we made often. And for goodness' sake, you could even put a scoop of ice cream in them if you wanted. After you finish the mac and cheese of course. I'm not a monster.

These white plates (plowls) were used day after day, time and again, through different cities and stages of our life. The more we stayed at hotels, the more adapted we became to living simply, with nothing but those plates, a microwave, and a tiny amount of groceries that fit in the mini fridge. For some reason those plates became a symbol to me of all the things I loved about living out on the road. I loved it being just Kyle and me, exploring a new city, meeting new people, and cooking chicken nuggets in a microwave for dinner. That was it. Nothing more than that. I had him, I had adventure, I had people, and it made me very, very happy.

A few years later, we were a bit out of the season of our hotel living way of life and more into our normal life kinda-an-adult-but-still-feel-young groove, and I came across those white plates, tucked away high in our cupboard, and I had a spiritual revelation.

---

[3]If Shakespeare can invent words at random, so can I.

A plain white plate from the dollar store gave me a divine insight. Dramatic, I know. But you don't get to choose where these types of messages from God come from, so let's dive right in.

I was in my kitchen doing that disgusting thing called "feeling sorry for myself." I was trying to talk myself out of it, truly, but it was not working and instead my brain was just playing the comparison to others game, majorly. I was feeling sorry about my frumpy house, our slender bank accounts, and all the stuff we didn't have. I would say things like, "But you own a home—even if it has ugly countertops, at least you own it! You have a husband! We have health—health is something, right? You have a job that pays you money to talk about books all day!" These were the sunshine rays trying with all their might to ward away my rain clouds of gloom and jealousy, but they were failing miserably. Which, of course, made me feel even worse about myself in this moment of pity-party disarray. Oh, so you can't even pep talk yourself into happiness? No, internal mean Aunt Karen, I can't. And you know what? Whenever someone says to "choose happiness," I want to slap them with a smiley face balloon across the face because if it were that easy of a choice, we would all be selecting that option, always. Duh. Sometimes it is more complicated.

I can see now the reason I was spiraling was that my focus had, for some time now, been securely fixed on what we did *not* have instead of all we did. We had just spent some time with friends at their gorgeous new home. It was big, it was new, it was everything our tiny townhome was not. Everything there was spacious and bright. Our home had tan carpet and 1980s cream-colored laminate countertops we couldn't afford to replace. The backyard was a small brick patio with a moldy fence around it the HOA promised to fix but never did. And we had only two

bedrooms. TWO! The horror. I wanted more. I wanted a home
that had a nice yard and new furniture not covered in mystery
stains. I wanted more money in my bank account, to be quite
frank. I wanted more square footage, more HomeGoods splurges,
more more more. I was drowning in wanting wanting wanting. I
wanted what *others* had—or at least appeared to have on social
media—and I couldn't even see all that God had given us right
here and now, and my soul smelled like old grocery store sushi
because of it. For so long I had been fixing my eyes on the wrong
things. We were so far separated from our time on the road when
we happily lived with little. We had roots now, a little mortgage,
furniture that didn't belong to La Quinta Inn. One would think
having more—stability, stuff, crap—would feel better. But it didn't.
All I could see was where I was lacking and not the abundance of
blessings right in front of my crinkled-up face.

While I was moping, I was also putting away dishes, which, to
be honest, was probably half the reason I was cranky in the first
place. Dishes are the worst. As I put away my large stack of
plates—far more than any two human beings would need—I saw
high on the shelf, pushed toward the back of our dusty shelf,
those sturdy, white, big-lipped dollar store plates that had carried
us faithfully through so many seasons. And it all came rushing
back instantly.

I remembered what it was like when those bowls were all we
really owned, yet we felt so rich. I remembered the freedom of
having less. The beauty of experiencing new places and meeting
new people, not buying more things and acquiring more junk. My
mind went back to the smell of hotel room coffee brewing as we
lay in the bed and watched cable TV we were not paying for. My
mind went back to the amazing taco shop we discovered in Dallas

or the hot bowls of pho we had in Seattle as it rained outside the restaurant window. My mind went back to how hard I would laugh with the friends we met who quickly became like family, and the precious memories we created with them. I remembered how Kyle and I had nothing but each other, a rented room, and a few tiny possessions yet felt so full of life, blessed, and so happy.

Please hear me on this. Having a home you love or wanting a better home to raise your family in and being financially responsible are good things. There is nothing wrong about setting goals, working toward them, and carving out the life you want in that way. But for me, it was all I was seeing, and that did nothing but pull my soul down into the muck.

The thing I feel is most important is perspective. Because without perspective, you could have a gigantic house, a super fancy-pants SUV, nine million dollars, and fourteen dachshund puppies and still want more. You would still be wanting what your neighbor has—twenty English bulldog puppies and ten million dollars. You would still be just wanting wanting wanting and not *living* along the way. And that is a dangerous, and not fun, cycle to live in.

So, right there, as I leaned on my eighties laminate countertop that looked like it could have once adorned a highway rest stop bathroom sink, I vowed to not spend my life stuck in the "jealousy, want, get, still be sad" vortex of life. I vowed to fill my life with things that couldn't be ordered via Amazon Prime but things seen, experienced, and hugged. I vowed to find joy in God and people as best as I could. Joy in my family and the friendships we intentionally form. Joy even when we don't have a lot, and joy when we do. Joy fueled by the things in life that are free. Because I love me some free stuff.

One day, I hope we will have a time when we need to pack up those white dollar store plates again and hit the road. I hope, even as we get deeper into adulthood, parenthood, and mortgage payments, we will continue to live a bit outside the lines of the norm. That we will continue to go on adventures, do our art that makes our hearts beat faster, and spend late nights laughing with new friends in new cities. I hope to keep living simply yet so full of gratitude each and every day. Because that, to me, is rich.

CHAPTER ELEVEN

LEARN TO LEAVE THE PAST IN THE PAST. EVEN IF IT INVOLVES CHRISTMAS COOKIES BEING LESS DELICIOUS

The harder we focus on how things used to be, the harder it feels when things change. And guess what? Things are *always* changing. So learning to be open to that change saves a lot of heartache.

And guess how I learned this? Christmas and flying snow shovels. Ho ho ho, friends.

The deeper Kyle and I got into full-blown adulthood, the more and more going home to Minnesota for Christmas felt different and required an adjustment of our expectations. When we were in college, the holidays still had a bit of that magic to them. Our families did the same traditions we had done since we were little kids. We would still take a whole day and bake a million sugar cookies, using the same cookie cutters we had used since I was five. We would spread the cheap canned white frosting on them and pile on sprinkles and dried-out Red Hots left over from the year before that were so rock hard that if you bit directly into one you would crack a tooth. The tree would be covered in the tackiest decorations, all of them so beloved. Our strings of goose, train, and chili pepper Christmas lights we had for years, the ornaments from our past family vacations, and the little Popsicle-stick mangers we made at Sunday school a decade before.[1] The tree wasn't exactly magazine spread–worthy, but it was full of memories, and unpacking each thing to hang up brought so much joy.

Even throughout college, "Santa" or some other mysterious creature would sneak into my parents' home and leave a stocking full of the same things every year: an apple, an orange, Hot Wheels cars, nuts with the shells on that required a nutcracker, a variety of chocolates, and a little book full of Life Savers.

And of course we would go to church together. We would sing the Christmas hymns, and they would turn the lights off for the final song as we all held candles, the white wax dripping and burning your hand without fail.

The sameness and traditions of the holidays are what make the season feel so magical. But life is constantly evolving, and sometimes it becomes too hard to hold on to the way things once were as they grow into something new.

It was my sophomore year of college that things really began to feel different. When I arrived home, exhausted from the journey and my cheeks red from the cold weather I was no longer used to, I noticed the tree right away. Nowhere to be seen were those goose and chili pepper lights. Now my mom decorated it like, well, a non-tacky person. Only white lights and matching

---

[1] Let this be known this is the best Christmas light combination of all time: geese, trains, and chili peppers. Take note this December, Joanna Gaines.

glass bulbs, and the only ornaments from our memory-filled stash allowed to see the light of day were ones that contained neutral shades. Gone was my glitter snowflake with rainbow sparkles on it—way too loud apparently. The tiny gold rocking chair could stay, however. It was a rough year to be any sort of festive decor under the wrath of my now neutral-shade-obsessed mother.

And then the cookies. Apparently I had developed a gluten allergy. Sigh. So gone were our rows and rows of sugar cookies, and instead we had a small batch of dough made from almond flour that would crumble apart if we attempted to use a cookie cutter, so we were forced to make them into little boring balls. The cheap Betty Crocker frosting did make the cut, however, and we piled it on thick to mask the dry sadness of the pathetic almond lump it adorned.

And then there was the stocking situation. We woke up Christmas morning, and the obnoxious, red velvety sock was hanging there empty. Not even one Hot Wheels car to be found.

"Oh, no stockings this year?" I asked my parents as they filled up their coffee cups.

They looked at each other, then my dad casually looked into his mug like a guilty puppy.

"We didn't feel like making another trip to the store," my mom said. "Plus, you're too old now anyway." Wow, Mom. Define *old* for me, would ya?

That year we opened our gifts and went to church and ate our Christmas ham and fruit salad, but I knew things wouldn't be the same as they used to be. And I was right—each year after that seemed to be further and further away from the Christmases I experienced growing up. And the point of this isn't just to whine about not getting a sock full of uncrackable nuts anymore. I can live without the nuts. It is just that the older and more "grown-up" I got, the more I would yearn for the things of the past. I know I am not alone in that.

When things got stressful in my day to day, I just wanted to go back to *that* time of life. One where things seemed a bit more magical and I could count on the sameness of it all. I wanted to feel the comfort in that, even if only for a few weeks of the year at the holidays. That had to be the fix all for life's grown-up problems, right? Returning to what you knew to be good and safe. Because nothing else was slowing down this responsibility train that kept speeding along with each passing birthday. When I was neck deep in the blah-ness of tax paying or job hunting or Comcast calling, I would daydream about bellying up to my family table to stuff myself with our traditional meal of tuna casserole topped with American cheese slices—fresh from the plastic wrapper.[2] This processed pot of bliss would be a precursor to a lovely evening watching those terrible yet amazing Claymation Christmas movies where Rudolph moves so jaggedly that he looks like a robot with a bad rust problem. Surely that would make everything right again. I just wanted home to stay the same and be a place of simple comfort and familiarity. And I wanted there to be a lot of plastic-wrapped American cheese involved because that always helps.

But instead, it became a place where I was slapped in the face with change. Everything in our life seemed to be different, including the place we knew for so long as home, and it was a hard concept to embrace. Also, I eventually developed an allergy to dairy as well as gluten, so there was that. No more tuna casserole

---

[2] "Bellying up" is a fun thing to say.

either and no more American cheese slices unless they came from the vegan section of the grocery store, were made out of coconuts, and cost approximately $35.

One year in my midtwenties, we decided that we were not going to go over to my aunt's on Christmas Eve like we had almost every year prior. My extended family had other things going on, so it was just my sister and me and our husbands at our parents' house together for the evening.

Since it was such a small group, the Canadian Club whiskey was poured early, and we settled in to open gifts—because why not?[3] There was nothing else going on. When we were kids, my family would go overboard with presents—stacks and piles of Fisher-Price and then later, when we were teens, CDs we begged for and tacky and shamefully overpriced Abercrombie sweaters we would end up exchanging anyway. This year, we adhered to the new adult standard of one gift per person. Sigh. So reasonable, so responsible. Most of the gifts were kitchen-related items, because apparently that is what adults give each other. Listen, now in my thirties I can certainly appreciate a full set of Pyrex glass food storage containers. That is a straight-up luxury. In my twenties, not as much. We all opened our one gift, and my mom made an announcement. Apparently there was one tradition we were still keeping. My mom had saved the largest present for the evening for last as a grand finale of gift-opening excitement, something we had always done. This year it was for my dad.

We all headed outside; the air was piercing cold, and the sky was clear and full of white, sparkling stars glittering off the snow and ice that blanketed everything around us. There was a sense of

---

[3]Gross. Why did we drink that? Here is a change for ya to embrace—stop drinking cheap whiskey named after Canada. Ron Swanson would be appalled.

calm and peace . . . until we all got out there. Fueled by our Canadian Club and the fun of revealing this big gift for my dad, we were cheering and shouting, guaranteed to be annoying every neighbor on our block, but we didn't care as it was Christmas, and there was fun to be had.

Kyle and my brother-in-law went into the corner of the garage where my mom had them hide the gift earlier that day, and they rolled it out. Our screams and cheers escalated as my dad gazed at his present: a snowblower. My dad had lived in Minnesota for more than fifty years and until now had cleared the driveway with a simple shovel. Now he had a beast of a machine that dramatically ate snow and spit it out into the sky with a loud rumble, which made this terrible winter chore not only more efficient but also exciting. Why it took so long for my parents to purchase such a helpful and practical item, I don't know. Probably the same reasons they didn't buy a microwave until the late nineties—they keep things simple and do whatever they want. But they now owned a snowblower, finally, and that was something to celebrate.

We were literally dancing around the new machine, hooting and hollering and being ridiculous, and tiny snowflakes began to fall. One of us had the great idea to find every snow shovel in the garage and throw it as far away into the yard as possible in a gesture of "see you later, you inferior snow-moving piece of crap." We were all throwing shovels, and I was laughing so hard I was crying, the tears of course immediately freezing to my cheeks.

I was standing there with a huge grin on my face and snow falling all around when it hit me. Not a flying shovel, but a revelation. Yes, Christmas was now different than it had been growing up. Really different. Everything about life was different.

But different doesn't always have to mean bad. In fact, different can mean good. Adulthood did bring a bunch of lame-o stuff, but it also brought about a lot of new opportunities to have fun. New ways I can connect with my family that I never would have wanted to do when I was seventeen and just wanted to go see my friends. This new stage of life brought a book of fresh pages to write memories in with my family, together, as adults. Memories like this one of throwing shovels across our yard, dancing and cheering under the dark purple, star-covered Minnesota sky.

I also realized that to fully enjoy this new chapter of my life— a.k.a. accepting I was an adult and there was no going back to a stocking full of Hot Wheels cars—I was going to have to let go of the way things used to be. At least a little bit. Because trying to hold on to something that will never return or be the same was getting me nowhere, except disgruntled, like an unsatisfied Walmart customer. If I loosened my grip on the past a bit, perhaps I would be able to fully grasp the good stuff all around me and ahead of me.

Change is hard for me. Anybody else? Normally to change something in our life that we have been used to or dependent on for a long time, Kyle has to just forcefully remove it or swap it out, whether it be an old car we have outgrown or an ugly chair I never really liked anyway but bought because it was cheap. Kyle removes it, I go, *oh, that wasn't so bad*, and then I enjoy the new goodness in front of me a little better.

Change is hard, but I do believe if we trust in God, we can trust that change—no matter how big, scary, and unknown it is—will be good. That God has us right in his hand and wrapped fully in his love as we transition into new seasons. So now, whenever I enter a new chapter of life, I enter it with open palms, to put it in the most hippie way possible. Actually, let's get even more hippie and out there—I start it with open palms facing up to the sky, releasing the way things were with gratitude and getting ready to accept whatever is to come.[4]

Thank you, God, for change and for pushing me out of the bounds of what I know to walk into something better. To let go of what I am comfortable with, to gently nudge me into what you know is best. And whatever that is, I know I can trust it will be great.

---

[4]Sorry, is this way too woo woo for you? It definitely sounds like something I picked up in a yoga class. But you get it, right? Be open to the new, let go of the old. The end. Now light some incense, bang a meditation gong, and move forward.

PART FIVE

MARRIAGE + FRIENDSHIPS

Hey there. I love my husband very much, but alas, I am nothing more than a meager, messy human being, as is he. Sigh. That means it can be *rough* at times. Ya know, two people, trying to be humans, together. Yes, a lot of times it is nothing short of amazing! I am so grateful for his love, his jokes, how he cares for me so well. But also, nobody has seen the worst of me like he has. And that's scary. It's vulnerable. And sometimes it's shameful on my worst of days. Listen, whether you are married or not, don't stop reading here. What we can all glean from this part is that humans are *so* flawed. Yet we still need to somehow function together successfully. The end. That narrative will never change. The amount of grace we need to give to ourselves and the ones we love is about . . . 900,000 pounds. Like eighteen buses full of muscly people on their way to a CrossFit competition—that is how much grace we need to give each other. I hope that whoever you love, you will keep fighting for that relationship, and not only consistently and healthily forgive them but forgive yourself when things get regrettably messy. It is worth it. The people we love are always worth it.

CHAPTER TWELVE

MAKING MARRIAGE WORK IN A 400 SQ. FOOT APARTMENT

G rad school was over. Our summer in the tiny Minnesota river town of Winona wrapped up. It was time to make our move. You know the one—the "big move to the big city" adventure that is the opening plot for so many romance films. New York, here we come, fueled on optimism, dreams, and the promise of a lot of Dunkin' Donuts in our near future. Texas was void of Dunkin', bless their hearts, and I missed it dearly.

Kyle and I were again doing the thing that at this point we were near pros at. Selling most of the things we owned and packing everything else up. This time it wasn't just into our little Toyota; we also got a small moving pod. Crazy, right?

We made the cross-country trip just fine, like always. Kyle did 98 percent of the actual driving, and because of that I allowed him to play as many hours of Harry Potter audiobooks and musical theater songs as he wanted in penance. I really hate driving; he really loves it. He also happens to love the cast recording of *Legally Blonde*, so bend and snap, folks. Whatever keeps you awake and happy in the driver seat, I accept it.

But as we approached the city and had a full view of the seemingly endless number of skyscrapers ahead of us, you better bet I changed the music to play "Empire State of Mind" by Alicia Keys. Cliché, I know, but I think all moves to New York have an element of cliché to them. I also played "New York, New York" by Frank Sinatra, of course. Kyle, feeling the looming stress of figuring out our new life and the brunt of the eighteen-hour drive we just completed, was not amused. But I was. I was so excited for our next chapter, to live in a city where there were countless songs sung about it because it was that big and exciting. My new home came with its own soundtrack, and you better believe I leaned hard into that as I walked the concrete jungles where dreams were made of.

Living in New York had been a dream of mine for so long. When I was in Austin watching people in ten-gallon hats ride their horse to the bar, I was dreaming instead of horses pulling carriages in Central Park while the Naked Cowboy strolled nearby.[1] That was the city I wanted. Not for its meandering nearly nude men but for its vast amount of art, culture, and opportunities. I wanted to take writing classes and meet people in my field and learn and grow in that way. But I also wanted to have endless city adventures with Kyle, each weekend with an unlimited amount of possibilities for us to explore and do. I wanted to fill up on the buzz and energy New York gave you from just walking down the street. I was so excited for Kyle and his agent to see where that would take him, and for both of us to dive fully into pursuing our passions and dreams during this precious time

---

[1] He still exists and does the whole Naked Cowboy thing, and that is simultaneously terrifying and amazing. Also I just googled him. He ran for president in 2012 and is officially sponsored by Fruit of the Loom. Highly recommend his Wikipedia page.

in our life where we were so blessed to have the opportunity to do so. I wanted New York, and as we got deeper into the city and the buildings got taller and taller around us, I was hoping the city would want me back.

We had found an apartment on the third floor of a brownstone walkup. Sounds fancy, but guys, listen up. We couldn't even afford to live in Queens, which was at the time the most affordable of the five boroughs. So, we had to go to what they call the "sixth borough" of New York City—Jersey City—to be able to find anything that fit our itsy-bitsy budget. A lot of die-hard NYC folks would turn their nose up at this, because although it was far closer to Midtown Manhattan than Brooklyn or even the Upper West Side, it technically was in New Jersey. But so many of my favorite people were born and raised in the Dirty Jerz, as they affectionately call it, so I didn't let this small label snafu deter me from having an awesome apartment we could (kinda) afford. It even came with a beautiful view of the One World Trade Center and Manhattan skyline. We were right there in the midst of it all, just not on the "cool" side of the river.

But I loved Jersey City, everything about it. At that time it was very much in an "up-and-coming" phase, and I love anything up-and-coming. Those cities and neighborhoods are always exciting to live in. Every week a new bookstore, coffee shop, or restaurant was popping up. It was full of culture and diversity, and ancient, gorgeous churches lined the streets of our neighborhood with huge rose windows and towering steeples. Plus, it had a perfect Dunkin' Donuts that sat right next to the train, which is very important.

The commute into Manhattan was clean, fast, and easy. It took Kyle about twenty minutes to get to Midtown for his auditions, which in New York City travel time is a dream. Our apartment also sat next to a gorgeous circular park that was blooming with flowering trees in the spring. There was a tiny, mostly empty library right around the corner that I would walk to. They always had the best new books and bestsellers available to check out, which made me concerned if anyone in Jersey City was reading books, but I accepted the gift from the universe. We also lived right next to the perfect, crowded, dirty, odd bodega—the best kind—where we could get anything we needed in a pinch. Would we have to dust off the jar of mayo before opening it? Yes. But it was still good, and much easier than trekking several blocks to a bigger grocery store.

Our little piece of the big city hustle was everything I had dreamed and hoped it would be. Well, except for one thing. One small issue, which turned out to be big. When I said "our little piece" of the hustle, I meant it. Our apartment was tiny. Four hundred square feet, to be exact.

Despite its size, it was a gorgeous space. Kyle and I both said "we'll take it" almost instantly when the realtor first showed it to us. He gave us a really weird look, but when we like a place, we know it and are always on the same page. The apartment had high ceilings, a gorgeous antique fireplace, and a cozy bay window with a view of the Manhattan skyline.

There was one long hallway that brought you to the bathroom, then at the end our bedroom that had a single square window overlooking the back of surrounding apartment buildings and a bunch of fire escapes, with the occasional pigeon for a bit of excitement. Ah, paradise.

Our kitchen had about two cupboards in it, which was enough space to store our cups, plowls, and canned goods. So one of the first things we did to settle in was buy hooks to hang all of our pots and pans on, all the way up the wall. Need to sauté something? No problem. Let me grab the ladder and get climbing.

It was a bit ridiculous, us suddenly finding ourselves as tiny home dwellers before tiny home living was trendy. But the small size didn't scare us. We had lived in cramped places before just fine—like the La Quinta Inn and Suites, remember? And our first home, which was just a little hut built into an old garage. We thought we would fare just fine. Would Waffles become a bit more obese with his limited roaming room? Likely, but we would just buy him diet cat food and call it a day.

But there was something we didn't really anticipate would shake up our cozy living quarters. Unlike before, when Kyle was spending most of his time at school or the theater, and I was still working in an office in Austin, this time we would not just be living together in a tiny home. We would also essentially be waking up together, working together, cooking together, sleeping together, trying to relax together (*trying* is the key word here), and then waking up and doing it all over again, day after day after day after day. Which was a lot of time together, especially when even if you went to opposite ends of your home from each other, you could still hear, maybe even smell, the other person.

Yes, Kyle had his agent and made trips into the city frequently for auditions or to meet with him. But I was still working full time from home as a book publicist. And when Kyle wasn't schlepping it to Manhattan, he was also home, doing a computer-based job to fill in the gaps between shows and gigs. Basically, instead of being a waiter as he got his shows lined up, he was able to work from the couch. Which was such a blessing! Except I was also on that couch. That tiny, little couch in our tiny, little, suddenly suffocating apartment. And because we were in New York, everything was insanely expensive, and I couldn't afford a co-working space. And there were only so many days in a week you could go to the coffee shop and buy a $7 gluten-free breakfast bar and then work for eight hours without feeling like every employee there wanted to "accidentally" drop their heaviest book on my head while stocking shelves for being such a lingering patron.

At first we were getting along fine with our new cramped routine, but things really started going south for us with the questions—typical marital questions about bills that needed to be paid, dinner plans, upcoming trips. It was horribly distracting but seemingly impossible to avoid during the workday. One person would ask a question—okay, fine, a normal thing to do. Then the other person would ask a question—okay, fine, but now we are just very off-track and both a little annoyed. More questions would be asked because we were surrounded by our entire universe and it was impossible to separate from these things. Like should I thaw chicken or beef for dinner tonight? We needed to make this decision pronto before our adequate thawing window dissipated. CHICKEN OR BEEF? Or the mail would arrive and with it some cute unexpected bills. So obviously that would be discussed. Or one person would want to watch television while they worked, but the other one didn't, so that was fun.

We were just two people sitting there in a too-small living room doing boring jobs with nothing but boring stuff to discuss, and it just was gross. And did I say boring? It was boring. And also gross.

Then there was the issue of the bathroom. When your living room/office/kitchen was just a few feet away from the john, there was no privacy. Every gas explosion, splish, splash, or plop could be heard, and no marriage should ever have to endure that sheer level of disgusting horror. Horror, I tell you. HORROR.

But the turkey sandwich–eating was the final straw. Kyle began wearing noise-canceling headphones—smart man—and they worked so well they also canceled out his ability to hear himself chew, bless his cute little heart. But I heard it, loud and clear. At first I didn't say anything. My default way of handling things is to try and just let things roll off my back, but that technique can backfire if you aren't careful. And these turkey sandwich lip smacks were not sliding off all that well anyway. After a few days of lunch hours from hell, I lost it.

"Your chewing—I have never heard such terrible chewing, when did you start CHEWING like that? I can't do this anymore," I ranted, dramatically throwing my hands in the air and pacing in a three-foot circle because that is all the room I had to pace. "I'm done. DONE." I had officially reached my max capacity for living, working, eating, pooping, cooking, sleeping, and existing in a tiny space with another human being, with nowhere to go to escape.[2]

I was in full-on wife rage mode, which, unfortunately, happens sometimes—I am an emotional person. But I hate it every time it does, regret it after, and am constantly working on reining in the drama a bit. At some level I knew that it wasn't about the sandwich-chewing but the big move we just endured, having to start our lives over again, tight finances, new routines, and, of course, being crammed together like sardines twenty-four hours a day. Though I loved a lot of it, the stress of living in New York was growing like Slimer in *Ghostbusters* and taking over everything.

I continued stomping around our miniscule space like a pissed-off minotaur in tap shoes, trying desperately to release the large

---

[2] Oh hellloooo Katie, it is me—Katie from the year of 2020. Just wanted to let you know that if you thought THIS was spending too much time inside with your loved ones, BUCKLE UP BABY. MUAHAHAHA.

amount of anger I felt through our old floorboards apparently. Sorry, below neighbors. Kyle, in the very frustrating way he always does, remained calm. He slowly finished his sandwich and grabbed his keys like he was leaving.

"Where are you going?" I snapped. He didn't even respond, just walked out without saying a word.

We have never been a silent treatment couple. If there is an issue, we discuss and move on. But he just cold shouldered me so hard, it stung.

As the scuffed apartment door shut behind him, I sat on our sagging Bob's Discount Furniture couch surrounded by dirty lunch plates, stared blankly at our antique fireplace with his still-glowing laptop on it, and wept. Ugly wept, per usual. The beluga whale was back. I wept over the amount of disgust I felt toward Kyle and how disgusted that made me feel about *myself.* I had never felt like this about him before. Sure, we'd had our fair share of fights, but this was a lingering staleness, which almost was more concerning. It seemed we were constantly mad, arguing, or just blah and tense, and I had no idea how to fix that. What used to be so easy and fuzzy and warm felt difficult, cold, and bitter.

Our childhood love story felt buried deep beneath the crust and stress of adulthood, and for the first time in my life, I worried it would never resurface. And I worried that I hated him, to be frank. That thought had never once crossed my mind before—he was my *person.* The one who made everything in life sweeter, funnier, comfier, and feel like home, no matter where we were together. And now, I was ranting because of the way he chewed his stupid sandwich and questioning if I hated him, and it freaked me out. This was a whole new territory for our marriage, one that

I would have much rather avoided altogether, yet we were walking right through it, squished tight by our apartment walls and the giant high-rise buildings that surrounded us.

Minutes turned into hours of him being gone, and he wasn't answering my calls or texts. I knew it was intentional, but did I let that stop me from trying again and again to get a response? Nope. When I am mad, it is impossible for me to remain quiet. Well, when I'm happy, the same thing happens. Basically there are always words coming out of my mouth during any emotion. But Kyle didn't answer, and this was in the era before I discovered the Find My Friends app, so I just sat and waited, wondering where he was and when he would be back in our tiny, cramped apartment that now felt hollow and oh-so-lonely.

Hours later, when the sun was setting, he returned. He walked in, and I instantly saw he went to where any sensible small space–dwelling creature would go in a time of marital crisis: IKEA.

Under his arm was a box for a mounted desk that would screw right into the wall and could be folded down and hidden behind a curtain when we were not using it. It actually was the same collapsible kitchen table we had when we were first married in our little garage. Fold it out for a table, fold it down for a funny-looking chunk of wood hanging on your wall, but more space to move around. He hung it under our small, square bedroom window so we could work in separate rooms when we needed a bit more room to spread out.

It was the most romantic piece of office furniture ever to exist.

I would set up my computer, crack open our little window, feel the salty air from the nearby Hudson, and hang out with a bunch of pigeons that decorated the fire escapes and neighboring roofs as I worked in peace, and I loved it.

Just having that small bit of separation helped us immensely. And we had a no-drama, straightforward talk about what we needed to do to make our new tiny life work out. We made basic ground rules to respect each other and keep our work life and married life separate, which is such a healthy thing to do. So, from nine to five Kyle and I treated each other less as husband and wife and more like coworkers. We untangled our limbs, stepped back, took a breath, and both felt so much better because of it. We talked less during the workday, I invested in noise-canceling headphones (because duh—why didn't I do that all along?), and I would work in the back of the apartment, and him in the front. When things still felt too cramped, I went and hid in the neighborhood coffee shop, bought my overpriced yet delicious breakfast bar, and avoided eye contact with the workers for as long as possible.

Kyle and I did what we had to do to make it work, gave ourselves grace on the days when it didn't go as smoothly as we would have liked, then picked back up and tried to do better the next morning. In marriage that is all you can do in any circumstance. Whether you live in a tiny apartment or a mansion, when you weave your life so tightly with another person, threads are going to come loose from time to time. And stepping back for perspective will help you have the energy to sew them back together again. That is all you can do. Day by day, grace upon grace upon grace, keep trying to weave the loose threads back in, and then enjoy each other as much as possible along the way.

At the end of our workday, I would fold the little desk down and pull the curtain shut. My commute home would be walking from the bedroom to the kitchen. Rush hour traffic would consist of my cats blocking my path in the hallway. Then Kyle and I would both tuck our laptops in a basket to signify the workday was over, and take a breath. We would climb the ladder, take a pan off the wall, cook dinner, and search real estate listings for a two-bedroom apartment. Eventually we found our stride and learned that sometimes a bit of space can bring you closer together after all.

CHAPTER THIRTEEN

LEARN TO TRUST GOD'S PROVISION WHEN YOU ARE BROKE LIKE A JOKE

When we managed to get out of our apartment, living in New York City was a beautiful experience. All around us was art, energy, and excitement. The ability to walk to the New York Public Library's main branch in Manhattan on a Saturday afternoon and be swept away by the sheer grandeur of it amazed me. And it was just a public library! There were odd people looking up questionable things on the public internet, surrounded by architectural excellence—only in New York. Some Sundays we would leave for church an hour earlier than normal and take the ferry across the Hudson to Lower Manhattan, the wind whipping our hair back as we turned our faces toward the sun. Every single time I marveled at the gigantic skyline in front of us that seemed to go on forever, as it never got old.

When we got off the boat, we would walk all the way to our church in Midtown, taking our time as we passed through neighborhood after neighborhood—Tribeca, SoHo, Greenwich, Chelsea—all wrapped in the golden early morning glow. The further we walked, the more they came alive with that New York City buzz as the city's quieter neighborhoods and side streets slowly woke up around us. I even loved taking the train home after late nights downtown with friends at restaurants or bars we would only go to once because there were millions more to explore after that. I would rest my head on Kyle's shoulder and close my eyes during the commute as the entire world seemed to whip by out the train window. I also loved our neighborhood's open studio art nights. Kyle and I would walk the dark city streets, hand in hand, and pop into a gallery for a free glass of wine and see all the creativity our little sixth borough had to offer.[1] I even kind of enjoyed the more challenging parts of living in the city, like learning how to grocery shop. Hot tip: when you are shopping by yourself and it's dark, cold, and rainy, it isn't the best time to purchase a twenty pound box of cat litter, which you then have to haul several blocks home and up three flights of stairs. But even with challenging cat litter mistakes, it all had a bit of magic and adventure to it.

Except for one thing. There was one thing that wasn't all that magical. And definitely not a fun adventure. Money, honey. We were broke in a way we had never been before. Dang it. Don't you hate it when that happens?

Sure, we had never been rich by any means. We got married very young, finished undergrad, then grad school, then jumped right into one of the most expensive places to live in the entire country, both of us working in the arts—all these things are the polar opposite of a get-rich-quick scheme. We were working more on the "good luck out there, bro" level. But we were well aware of

---

[1] Free wine is always the best wine.

our choices and were happy with them. Taking our chances on following our hearts, dreams, and what we felt God had called us to do always outweighed any sense of striving for a massive financial cushion under our butts. Because even then, in a "stable" job, sometimes that cushion could fall out from under said butt, and you find yourself starting from the ground up anyway.

Kyle and I were (mostly?) smart with our money. We budgeted and then tried our darnedest to stick to that budget. All our bills and needs were covered and paid right on time, but when you only have a little bit of money coming in and a lot of bills needing to go out, being smart doesn't get you all that far. New York City put us in a place where our monthly finances were so tight, any unexpected expense would put us in the red the next month. Medical bill? Car problem? Intense desire to drive to Sleepy Hollow over Halloween weekend because when else do you have that chance in life? Budget is blown to bits. Cool. Time to whip out the credit card, I guess.

In preparation for our move to New York and trying to make sure we could actually make it happen, I had become obsessed with Dave Ramsey and his money ways. But now, his cash-only life was sometimes just not an option for us, and I could feel him hovering over me like some big anxiety-causing budget banshee, tsk-tsking at me in shame every time I checked my meager bank account, or I felt him attempting to poltergeist-slap my wallet out of my hand whenever I tried to buy my Dunkin' iced coffee. *You have coffee at home, Katie. I know, Dave, but it tastes disgusting—you drink it! This $3 beverage is bringing me life right now, and that, I feel, is very worth it.*

I had this extra cloud of anxiety over me because I knew we were doing a lot of stuff he would yell about on his radio show, but

I didn't really see a way around it. God bless him, he does a lot of good and really did help us get heading in the right path with our money, but also, chill out bro. You are giving me night terrors.

When you are in your twenties and thirties, it sometimes feels like you are in a never-ending season of acquisition. You are always trying to get *something*. A spouse, a job, a home, a better home, more money, some friends, a baby, a car that doesn't break down every Saturday morning just to ruin your weekend, a new tube of wrinkle cream that you can afford and actually works. It's just a gathering and acquiring time of life, and when you feel like you are not gathering and acquiring as well as everyone you see on Instagram—otherwise known as the public portal of lies—it can feel soul crushing. The jealousy and comparison can creep in and take over so quickly, like thorny vines silently suffocating your joy as you scroll in bed in the morning, before even setting your feet on the ground for the day. Wow, that was dramatic. Thorny, soul-crushing vines of Insta-filtered doom. But you get it.

In New York, Kyle was getting acting jobs and doing his computer day job in between, and my full-time job was chugging along just fine, but fine and random didn't really cut it when we were paying so much for our apartment, our student loans, our own health insurance, or our weekly required sushi allotment—everything. You know, adulthood in all its glory. Paying for all of the things and then even more things. And then the unexpected things. And then paying for a few things you probably don't need, but you are just trying to enjoy life for a hot minute because you are stressed out from being so broke, so they become an essential item. Then you pay for those things a little bit more in the form of regret, shame, and credit card bills.

It all boils down to this: money was very tight. Plain and simple. So we were officially going through a time where we were forced to fully rely on God's provision. Ugh, how boring, right? An overflowing bank account just seems, to my little brain, a bit more comforting and fun, to be completely honest. But comforting and fun doesn't always grow your soul in the way it needs to grow. Boo. But true. Sometimes you need growth and growth is hard, so here we were. Broke and, I guess, growing.

Our "livin' on a prayer" season of life didn't even have an expiration date. We couldn't see a light at the end of any tunnels. Not even an iPhone flashlight to low-key guide us in the general right direction. So what do you do then? When you are in a place of struggle, of tangible, physical need, without a clear, easy way out of it?

When all my go-to comforts are stripped from me—a sense of physical and financial security, an understanding of what outcomes I can expect, my tangible needs and emotional needs being met—I have learned just to lean *hard* on God, with the expectation he will show up with enough to get me through. How? Just by the good ol' "cry out to God" method because sometimes that is all we have to offer.

For me that looks like blunt prayers—sometimes as blunt as, "God, help." Sometimes a bit more flowery. But I also do it through reciting Scripture. I had a client once who just whipped out appropriate Scriptures at any given moment, right in the middle of our calls or any other normal conversation, and it fascinated me. I needed some of those weapons in my arsenal. So just like I did at Grindstone Lake Bible Camp when I was a stinky preteen who had not yet discovered deodorant, I memorized Scriptures. Not a lot—there was no canteen candy prize incentive now like there was back at camp—but some. And some were better than none.

This was my first to memorize as an adult:

> Do not be anxious about anything, but in every situation, by prayer and petition, with thanksgiving, present your requests to God. And the peace of God, which transcends all understanding, will guard your hearts and your minds in Christ Jesus. (Philippians 4:6-7)

I love the part that his peace transcends all understanding. Because in the toughest and tightest times, sometimes that is what we need most. Supernatural peace that carries us through to when our ground is a bit sturdier. There have been so many times when I would pray—a.k.a. beg, cry, make my whale noises—to God, just asking for peace to make it through whatever difficult situation was before me. And sometimes it would show up, and to me that felt like a miracle.

But I also love that these verses tell us to present all our requests before God, like a boring version of *Total Request Live*. That we can have a full episode of TRL with God, don't even have to deal with Carson Daly, and are promised the peace of Christ that passes all understanding as a result is a pretty good deal.

And then there is this little ditty—my tried and true I have repeated to myself so many nights when I just needed to fall asleep peacefully and so desperately yearned to wake up with a heart full of hope and joy, not sheer terror and anxiety crusted onto my soul. Because waking up to stress and dread just gets so annoying, and nobody likes crust, except on pizza. And pies. Here it is:

> Let the morning bring me word of your unfailing love,
>> for I have put my trust in you.
> Show me the way I should go,
>> for to you I entrust my life. (Psalm 143:8)

Simple. Let the morning bring me word of your unfailing love, for I have put my trust in you. I love that. I *love* that mercies are new every morning, for all of us, no matter what. That something so spiritually wonderful and magnificent can happen overnight while you dream about hippos doing the Macarena is a beautiful thing. You can wake up with a bit more joy in your heart, and God can completely turn around your circumstances that at one point seemed un-turnaroundable.

And then there is this. Which, for the record, is very long and I have not fully memorized it—whoops. But I do often think of those little birds and how they are so provided for, and therefore we will be provided for as well. Hopefully our provision will come in a different way than discarded McDonald's french fries in a Walmart parking lot. But you go, birds—whatever tweets your tweeter.

> Therefore I tell you, do not worry about your life, what you will eat or drink; or about your body, what you will wear. Is not life more than food, and the body more than clothes? Look at the birds of the air; they do not sow or reap or store away in barns, and yet your heavenly Father feeds them. Are you not much more valuable than they? Can any one of you by worrying add a single hour to your life?
>
> And why do you worry about clothes? See how the flowers of the field grow. They do not labor or spin. Yet I tell you that not even Solomon in all his splendor was dressed like one of these. If that is how God clothes the grass of the field, which is here today and tomorrow is thrown into the fire, will he not much more clothe you—you of little faith? So do not worry, saying, "What shall we eat?" or "What shall

we drink?" or "What shall we wear?" For the pagans run after all these things, and your heavenly Father knows that you need them. But seek first his kingdom and his righteousness, and all these things will be given to you as well. Therefore do not worry about tomorrow, for tomorrow will worry about itself. Each day has enough trouble of its own. (Matthew 6:25-34)

I mean, come on. God provides daily for birds. BIRDS! He did it thousands of years ago and he does it now. Even the nasty pigeons on the fire escape outside my tiny bedroom window. In fact, not only does he provide for those birds, but he *loves* those birds. They always seem to have enough scraps of old hot dogs and pizza slices in New York, and fresh salty air to fly through over the Hudson. And if pigeons—also known as nasty rats with wings and freaky little beady eyes—have enough, perhaps we will have enough. He provides for pigeons in New York. He provides for deformed crows in Walmart parking lots, so I am betting he will provide for us too.

I have found it is in these times when you are at the literal edge of what you think you can endure, and all other comforts and backup plans and comfortable places to fall are stripped away, there is only one thing to do: Really examine if you believe God is who he says he is. And if you believe he will do what he has promised us time and again in Scriptures. That he will meet our material needs. And not only that but also our spiritual needs, which is just a lovely bonus. While we wait for a physical need to arrive, God's grace shows up by giving us enough strength every morning to get up and get through the day and have a little joy while doing so.

So in New York, when we were struggling with money and the burden of that was weighing on our shoulders, I would pray for God to bring his supernatural strength and peace to just get us through the day. I would remind myself God's mercies are new with every sunrise over the Hudson River, and his love for us is taller than any Manhattan high rise trying to block our view of the beauty. Plus, he loves dirty, ugly pigeons and therefore must also love me.

With no real path or option to change our circumstances and no other options, we relied on our faith in God to calm our anxious hearts and help us have enough to get by. I repeated those Scriptures, and then I forced my little pea brain to try and fully believe them. Kyle and I reminded each other of those promises of God and his new mercies that were sure to come. I truly believe that hope is always around the corner. Times can feel bleak and tight and not fun, but the good stuff usually shows up eventually. Not always on our time schedule, but it can be trusted to arrive, sometimes even busting into your life when you least expect it, throwing glitter in your face with fanfare while conveniently missing your sensitive corneas.

During this time of empty pockets but full prayer lives, we kept doing our part. Working hard, tithing, doing our absolute best at every single thing we had tangible control over, and then trusting God for everything else. And sometimes that is all you can do. New York was our crash course in trusting in God's provision, whether we wanted to or not. A time when our faith was tested, refined, and ultimately strengthened. And guess what? We didn't have a lot, by any means, but we always had enough. Always. And in that season, having enough was, well, simply enough.

CHAPTER FOURTEEN

WAIT FOR GOD TO OPEN THE DOOR FOR YOU. EVEN IF IT'S A DIFFERENT DOOR THAN YOU EXPECTED

I feel like the biggest marital fights always happen on the way to church. I don't want to get all creepy spiritual about it, but perhaps it is the devil being a big ol' jerk and trying to throw you off the path of having a peaceful morning worshiping God. Or from even getting to church altogether. It's either that or the fact it's early, and Sunday mornings can be difficult for anyone to get dressed and out the door to get somewhere at a certain time without getting a little bit cranky at their loved ones along the way.

I thought I was the only one who would get oddly mad at my spouse en route to the house of God, and I felt a lot of shame about it. Because when you let your anger get the best of you five minutes before you shake someone's hand with a big old smile on, then settle in to sing "How Great Thou Art," it just feels extra yucky. But then one day, one of my strong, blunt fellow Enneagram Eight pals blurted out she always gets *so* annoyed at her husband on the way to church, and I felt so vindicated in that moment. Don't you love those times? When you are like "oh, thank goodness it isn't just me messing up all the time." There is something so important in that, in remembering it isn't just me. And it isn't just you, either, for the record. Let this be your official reminder that if you mess up or are struggling or just feel like a big pile of blah, you are not alone. We are all walking through the muck; some just hide it a bit better than others. That's why it's so important to be open about your junk, so other people can offload their own junk. Everyone wins when we are honest with each other and are reminded that we are all just doing our best and sometimes that isn't too pretty. Sometimes it is, sure. But sometimes we more resemble a discarded box of salmon takeout on a hot New York City sidewalk. Stinky, visible, and just wrong.

Even though they occasionally happen to us—and I guess to a lot of married people—I hate pre-church fights. I hate any fight with my husband, of course. But the arguments on the way to church make me feel extra bad afterward. Still, they bubble up from time to time. That is what Kyle and I were in the middle of one Sunday morning as we exited the subway and began the half-mile walk to our church in Chelsea. No long leisurely walks through lower Manhattan this day, just a hustled rush off to service full of sharp words, sighs, and eye rolls. We were arguing with each other on a bustling New York City sidewalk, because if you are going to fight, you might as well make it as public as possible, right?

See, I had been trying to pry information from Kyle, and he was locked up tight, completely unwilling to let me know any tiny bit of what was happening emotionally inside of him. But I knew something was wrong. I could just tell something was *bothering* him, and deeply. He wasn't happy, and I was worried.

Kyle and I are so different in the way we process hurt and frustration. When anything bothers me—and I mean anything— I have to verbalize it nine hundred times, over and over, until it feels less itchy to my soul, hence the reason I was continuing our squabble the entire way to church instead of setting my feelings aside until a more appropriate time. That is nearly impossible for me, unfortunately. Yet when something bothers Kyle, he just pretends it doesn't. The end. He has this tough old Nebraskan farmer "stuffing away his feelings until they just don't exist anymore" process for handling pain. It is borderline impressive, borderline concerning.

But I know him. I know what every tiny facial expression means. I can tell if he is stressed by the way he sits on the couch. If he walks around the house with his hoodie pulled up over his head, he is definitely not in a good place. I can tell if he is annoyed with someone at a party by the way he sips his drink and looks at them. I can tell if he had a bad day at work by the way he drives the car. And if I hear him singing from the next room I know he is doing great. I love when I overhear him singing; it makes everything feel better in the world. But I hadn't heard that for a few weeks now. He just felt off to me, but when I would ask, I would get nothing back. Just "I'm fine" and him trying to move things along, but I knew in my heart it wasn't, well, right. I was worried he was depressed and I wanted to help, which is both a good and very annoying quality for a person to have.

At some intrinsic level, despite not having a lot to go off of, I thought I knew what he was internally struggling with. But it was a big thing, something not easy to fix. If I was right, I knew asking him about it would just make him even more annoyed at me than he already was as we continued our last few blocks of walking. But again, the filter over my mouth is not the best, so I just went all in.

"Are you not happy living here?" I asked as we waited on a corner for the stoplight, with people crowded all around us.

He didn't even look at me as he denied it was the problem, his eyes firmly fixed on the crosswalk ahead of us. But I could tell that was it, as I suspected, by the way he clenched his lips shut after simply saying no.

Kyle and I both loved living in New York for the fun parts. The energy, the culture, the friends we had there, the endless places to explore and adventures we went on. The city lit us both up on the weekends. But on weekdays, not so much. I could tell Kyle didn't exactly love the whole "haul butt into Manhattan, sit in an over-crowded casting waiting room, audition for a weird casting director for two minutes, then go home and wait three weeks before hearing anything back from your agent, if at all." He didn't love his boring computer job, though he was grateful for it. But it was mind-numbing all the same. He loved acting, that was for sure. You can see his soul bubbling up and out of him when he's performing on stage. But I think our time in New York helped him realize he wanted more *control* over his art, and his life. And the whole "New York actor" way of existence was the polar opposite of having control. You are at the mercy of everyone else—waiting for that yes to come. Waiting for someone to pay you. Waiting for someone to even give you a shot in the first place. Yet there we were, living in the city. Doing the acting thing, the city-living thing we had worked so hard to do, yet now realizing it may not be what he really wanted after all, which is a hard thing to comprehend.

I have always encouraged Kyle to chase his dreams, and our move to New York was a big part of that. That is what you do, right? If you are an actor, you move to New York. But the big city adventure was also something *I* really wanted, so encouragement from me to "chase that dream, dude!" may have been coming on a little strong in that area. I was realizing that I had to take a step back and let him tell *me* what his dreams actually looked like, not carve them out for him in a way that seemed the most exciting and fun from my perspective. Ouch. A tough thing for me to realize, but so necessary.

So after months and months of just bending to the mercies of casting agents and his agent and the luck of the draw that comes with the acting gig life, he realized he hated it on a level deeper than he expected. Kyle, my stoic, strong dude who can fix or handle anything, was now in his own "stuck" season with no way out. I had no solution. He had no solution. The corner bodega owner had no solution. Waffles had no solution. We were in New York, doing the thing and, it turns out, hating it all the while.

It broke my heart to see Kyle stewing in his hurt. He seemed stuck in the mud, and being the fixer that I am, I really wanted to pull him out. But I couldn't. He wouldn't even let me try. And I know we handle pain differently, but it still doesn't mean I won't work with all my might to help him make things better for him, to a slight fault. Sometimes a big fault.

The last few minutes of our walk, by the grace of God, I finally shut my mouth and just began praying for him. It was one of those desperate, begging prayers. *Please God, help Kyle. Help him, please. I don't know how to help him. Help him, please. Help him.*

I didn't know *how* God would help him, or when. It seemed like there wasn't anything we could do to fix this cycle of frustration we were in, and that hurt my soul so deeply. I wanted Kyle to be okay, but I was not able to make him okay, and I wasn't even sure how he could make himself okay.

Please, God, just help, I asked one more time silently as we entered the old cathedral our church rented in the evenings for our worship service. We read the doxology, we sang our hymns. I remember nothing of the sermon, just the musty smell of the aging church as we sat on the scratchy red velvet pew and as I gazed up at the stained-glass windows trying not to cry. I was trying to look like a normal, "happy" married couple but knowing things were definitely not okay between us, and my heart was aching.

But sometimes God blindsides you in a way you could never expect or predict. As simply as we entered into that church full of despair and silent, desperate prayers, we left with a very tangible response from God. As soon as we hit the New York sidewalk again, Kyle glanced at his phone and there was a voicemail.

A few weeks back a former professor of Kyle's sent him a job opportunity in Memphis, Tennessee. The job would be to lead the theater department at an all-boys Catholic school full of a bunch of football bros. They paid well for being a high school, and it seemed like a cool opportunity to carve out a department and have a ton of creative control, all while making an impact in the lives of the boys. He told me about it and I said sure, apply, and didn't even think about it again until that moment, with that voicemail, on the sidewalk. It was the program director, who wanted to do an interview the next day. Just an hour after my desperate prayers, we seemed to have something that was an out. An out from the hurt Kyle was feeling, the frustration. A door opened when all we saw was walls, and I know that was only something God could do for us.

Kyle did the interview, and it went really well. This was turning into one of those situations when everything seemed to perfectly align, step by step, better than you could ever plan out or hustle into alignment by yourself. They told Kyle they wanted to fly us both out the next week to meet in person and for us to explore Memphis and see if it was a place we wanted to live. I had to do a deep Google dive about it, having zero knowledge except a vague idea that Elvis lived there at some point. While I knew nothing about the city, I did know my desperate prayers seemed to have been answered in record time. It's like I had put a prayer in the microwave and two-and-a-half minutes later I had a hot, steaming bowl of clarity. Never before have I had God in the span of a single church service change the entire direction of my life in such a visible, tangible—and eventually we would learn—good way.

We flew out the next week, taking a train, bus, and taxi to the disgusting Newark airport, and boarded our plane. When we landed, just like Kyle and I instantly knew we loved our sun-drenched brownstone apartment in Jersey City, we both instantly knew we loved Memphis. The old, gorgeous cracked buildings. The history. The important part it played in the civil rights movement. The culture. The grit and the soul of the blues music that played from restaurants and bars. We visited the funky midtown neighborhood of Cooper-Young and ate at a place called The Beauty Shop, which used to be where Priscilla Presley would get her beehive coifed. Now it was a swanky brunch spot, where we got the most delicious chicken and waffles and gigantic mimosas beneath a vintage hair dryer.

We walked hand in hand through the downtown streets with the crooked sidewalks that seemed to be full of stories from the past. I met a friend of a friend at a strange coffee shop named Otherlands, where every single table and chair was mismatched and they had a little shop in the back where you could buy incense, quirky gifts, and hippie-worthy clothing items. I was obsessed. Kyle and I walked the path next to the Mississippi River, the same river that went right through our hometown in Minnesota, and it all felt so new but comfortable at the same time. Memphis just had this *spirit* to it, this energy and excitement that we wanted more of. It wasn't the same energy of New York. It was slower yet powerful and simply fun. The music, the history, and of course the food. It had everything I loved about New York but in a smaller, more accessible form. Instead of observing art from the outside, there was more opportunity to participate in it yourself, and that excited me.

The final kicker was this: in my googling I learned Memphis at the time was the fourth cheapest city in America to live in. That also helped our decision. Because trying to survive in New York was not getting any easier without having a stress vein permanently popping out of our foreheads twenty-four hours a day. And nobody wants a stress vein. Gross.

Kyle did his in-person interview that weekend and loved it. The school, the program, all of it. He would have such creative control over his craft, which he and I both realized was what he wanted all along. Not to trudge into Manhattan in hopes someone would give him a shot. His personality was more in line with calling his own shots, making his own shows, and teaching others about the beauty of performing along the way.

So a mere nine months after our New York City move—a place we had planned on living and staying in indefinitely until God himself moved us—well, God did move us. Far sooner than expected. Our journey would take us from Minnesota to Florida to Texas to New York and now to Tennessee. We would yet again be moving, starting fresh, carving out another life for ourselves.

We packed up our Jersey City apartment, shipped our stuff in a pod ahead of us, and piled into our tiny Toyota. The last thing we did before leaving Jersey City was pull the little piece of paper that said "Schnack" out of our mailbox in the hallway of our small yet gorgeous brownstone apartment with the view of lower Manhattan from the living room. The apartment that taught us so much about each other in such a little space, in such a little amount of time. My heart hurt, but I also felt at complete peace. I knew God had completely orchestrated this move. Because it was never in our plans. Not even close to being in our plans. But sometimes, those unexpected plot twists are the best things that can happen to you in life. I knew without a doubt God would provide for us in Memphis. I knew he would bring us community and a home to live in, and give us more joy than we could ever have conjured up on our own hustling in New York. I didn't know how, but I knew he would, because this whole thing was his idea, not mine.

So we yet again got in our car stuffed full of our meager belongings. As we began yet another cross-country move, I grabbed Kyle's hand and smiled at him as he sang loudly to the radio, knowing deep in my heart we were going to be okay.

PART SIX

MENTAL MENTAL HEALTH, Y'ALL

Hey there. Anyone else struggle with mental health? Oh, just me? Cool. At least that is the lie I tell myself in my lowest moments. But over the past few years, as people have been working to erase this stigma of mental illness—thanks, internet, for your encouragement there—I have worked to be kinder to myself. I remind myself that no, I am not the only one who has ever had a panic attack before. This part shares a bit more about my journey with mental health and hopefully gives you a big warm hug and a nice cup of sunshine as you navigate any struggles you may be working through. I truly believe mental health problems are not personality problems. God isn't mad at you that you are anxious right now, or depressed, I promise. It is okay. God has a lot of love and grace to give you when it seems too hard to get out of bed in the morning or when you feel like you can't keep your head above the waters of worry. I hope you will keep fighting against whatever it is you are facing and ask God to show up, and then expect it with open arms.

CHAPTER FIFTEEN

SAY HI TO THE OLD LADY ON THE PORCH

Kyle and I made it to Memphis. After a few days of searching, we found our new apartment to rent. It was the bottom level of an old white house with a big front porch, stone fireplace inside, tons of windows, and creaking original wood floors. It was in a perfect location—we were right between the cute area of Cooper-Young, full of restaurants and coffee shops, and Overton Square, which had endless nightlife options full of live music and dingy Memphis dive bars. We were also close to Overton Park, a gigantic green space with a historic bandshell right in the middle, where Elvis Presley played his very first show when he was still in high school. They now have free outdoor concerts there four nights a week in the summer, and it seems all of Memphis shows up with their lawn chairs and coolers to enjoy local blues or folk musicians playing under the Tennessee sky.

When we visited Memphis for the interview, I had walked past a church downtown and wrote down the name in my phone and didn't really think much of it. Once we were settled, we checked it out one Sunday and fell in love, and quickly fell into their community and began meeting people. They met in an old, rundown historic church downtown, the Clayborn Temple, that was home to a lot of important moments in the civil rights era. It was at that church where they handed out the "I Am a Man" signs and gathered to march with Dr. Martin Luther King Jr. for the sanitation workers' strike. The church had seen some things and had this wonderful sense of history. It was also falling apart. They had nets up so pieces of the ceiling wouldn't fall on our heads during the service, and some of the big, floor-to-ceiling stained-glass windows were missing pieces. I couldn't help but enjoy the drama of it all. Will plaster fall on my head at church today? Possibly. Old, interesting, gorgeous, messy, and full of love. That was our church, and that was the whole city of Memphis really.

One thing I quickly noticed after moving to Memphis was how everything moved more slowly and had a sense of peace surrounding it. Well, everything except me. While the city carried on with its steady rhythm, I fell apart.

I have learned something about my mental health over the years since I started having anxiety and depression in Austin. During an extra stressful or difficult time, my body and brain rise to the occasion. The extra adrenaline seems to inflate me inside and helps me focus, stay on task, feel happier even—though it is a false sense of happiness. Is that healthy? Probably not. Because then, when things get calm, normal, how they should be, and life falls back into a regular pace, I crash. All that was filling me up exits my body, and I become a shell of sadness, anxiety, and leftover unresolved mental junk. The first time this happened, I was confused. Why am I a mess *now*? Things are finally going great! But then it happened another time, and I figured it out.

About six months after a very stressful or even traumatic time in life, my body "lets down" and my brain has a nuclear meltdown.

So, in Memphis, all the stress of moving to New York within the last year, trying to survive in New York, and then quickly doing yet another cross-country move was finally chipping away at me, and my mental health was a big ol' mess. My heart hurt deeply, and depression was weighing on me more heavily than it ever had before, and I felt I was drowning. Most nights I would be on the floor of the bathroom weeping. And, as I have said, I am not a quiet crier. One time after a particularly bad night, my upstairs neighbor checked in on me the next day, so that was awkward. I tried to cry more quietly after that.

It hurt to exist, to breathe, to do anything. Clearly I was struggling, big time. But this is how I know it wasn't just me being a pouty dork—I *wanted* the energy to enjoy our new life. I could clearly see on paper everything was lined up and going great! I was excited about where we were, about our new chapter. But I could barely function under the sadness that decided to blanket me anyway. It was so frustrating. In the morning, my one goal for the day was to make it to the coffee pot. Get a little work done. Try to hold off crying as much as possible. Repeat. I hated it. I hated being depressed. It felt like it was something holding me back from all I wanted to do, experience, see, accomplish. But there I was, in deep and fighting to get my brain right-side up again. How boring.

Kyle and I did my normal checklist of things to try and get my health back on track—exercise, keeping up on my medicine, trying to make friends, going to church, going for hikes on the weekend and trying to do fun things together in the evenings, blah blah blah. But I knew part of the problem was I was alone in this big house every day working by myself while Kyle was teaching at school. And I am a super extrovert. Human beings give me energy and joy—two things I had just about zero of. I missed seeing people—friends, coworkers, anyone really. I felt so isolated in this new city, in this new house, just looking at my email inbox every day.

So I joined a coworking space in Cooper-Young, the cute little neighborhood down the street. I had to force myself to sign up online, despite everything within me saying to hide in your home alone forever and be sad. Then I had to force myself to actually go there one day. It was all a lot of mental effort, but I knew I needed it. Kyle and I only had one car at this point, and his school was a twenty-minute drive away, so I was left to navigate my way around Memphis on my $50 Target bike. From the first time I went to the coworking space, I could tell it was going to help me. I talked to human beings. I drank a lot of free coffee and ate a lot of free snacks. I saw other human beings walking outside the sunny window on the sidewalk. I had lunch with a few other coworkers in the nearby restaurants, which was nice. And I couldn't burst into tears in the middle of a busy office, so that was helpful. Well, I could, but it would throw off everyone's work vibes, so I didn't. So every day I would get on my bike, put Bob Marley on my headphones, and bike to the coworking space, turning my face to the sun and trying to cocoon myself in some sense of happiness as best as I could.

It was only about a ten-minute ride to the office, so most days I would also bike home for lunch, then back in an hour later. Four times a day, back and forth, I would bike down the historic, tree-lined Memphis neighborhood streets with the cracked sidewalks and bumpy roads. And that is where I first saw her.

On the porch of a house covered in chipped white paint, on the corner of the street just one block from my coworking space sat an old lady. And by sat I mean she sat there *all* the time. She was there every time I biked past, early in the morning, back and forth for lunch, and home again for the evening. As everyone did in Memphis, she waved to me each time I passed by—a far cry from New Yorkers whose main goal in life is to avoid eye contact with everyone. So I waved back, because if a cute old lady waves at you and you don't wave back, you might be the biggest jerk ever to exist. But day after day, wave after wave, it began to feel weird to *not* stop and say hello. How many times can you wave and not actually speak without it getting awkward? And I was curious about her. Who was this old woman who sat on this porch in her rocking chair, her hands folded nicely over her stomach as she rocked, waved, rocked, waved? So one day, I stopped my bike and said hello.

"Sit down," she said immediately, and gestured to the empty rocking chair next to her. I was a little nervous, but she seemed kind. And she was old, so if she tried to murder me I could just push her over and run away.[1] So I sat.

"What's your name?" she asked.

"Katie."

"Katie, I'm Edna. I am ninety-five years old. Damn, I'm old," she said, her eyes crinkled with a smirk.

Up close, I could see every line on her pale face. Her white hair was short and wispy and stood out in odd spots. Her hands seemed strong yet soft, and I noticed she had nice nails with a layer of clear polish making them shine. Her eyes were bright blue,

---

[1] I watch too much Dateline.

and she had only one tooth in her mouth holding on for dear life to survive.

She kept rocking in her chair as she gazed peacefully out to the street in front of us and dove right in to filling me in on all the details of her life, like we were new and old friends all at once.

She told me she was from a tiny mountain town in Eastern Tennessee, where if someone in the community misbehaved or committed a crime, the men would throw them off a cliff to take care of business themselves. Sounds charming! She was the oldest of eight children, and they all lived in a trailer. Her mom died young and her dad was abusive. So when she was fifteen years old she decided she had enough. She went to the local preacher, he gave her ten dollars, and she took a bus to Memphis and never looked back.

She kept rocking and rocking in her wooden chair as she told me all this, her voice steady and showing no signs of regret, but owning her story with every word she spoke.

When she got to Memphis, she found a job working at a dry cleaner and began renting the apartment across the street. She eventually married, but her husband died when they were only twenty-eight years old from a heart issue. I was twenty-eight at the time, so it stung a bit extra to hear this. When she told me about him, her demeanor changed to that of someone clearly still harboring the pain.

After he died, she never remarried—or even dated. "I never wanted to," she told me. "A death like that can still make you ache after all this time," she said, her eyes glazing over with grief seemingly as fresh as it was nearly seventy years ago. "Plus, what would I do with some ol' man? They need something from you all day long, then they need something from you all night long too," she said, cackling.

"I began to work double shifts in a factory to support myself," she said. "I never had much, but I had enough." She had owned her home for decades, which now happened to be in one of the trendiest neighborhoods in the city. You could tell she had great pride in it. The yard was cut, she had fresh flowers planted— always yellow—and the porch was clean.

I asked Edna if she had family nearby. She told me she had her neighbor Monty. He would come check on her every single day. He was in his forties and lived with another man a few houses down. "They are just roommates—the prices of living are so *high* these days," she said, but I couldn't help but wonder if that really was the case. She told me how Monty would bring her food, take her to the doctor, even cut her nails and hair when she needed it. He did everything for her beyond what the state services provided. The only relation was they were neighbors.

She stopped rocking then, looked me straight in the eyes, and said, "I just take it one day at a time. That is all you can do. Take it one day at a time, and just do the best you can."

She repeated that same sentence to me the next day when I stopped by, and again the next day, and the next day, and the next. Just take it one day at a time, and do the best you can. Going to see her quickly became my favorite thing to do as we rocked and talked, and she repeated that mantra I so desperately needed to hear. She had no idea how her example of strength and frequent reminders to take it one day at a time and do the best you can were keeping me going during some of the hardest few months of my life.

But for as much old-timey stories and sage advice Edna doled out, she was full of jokes too. One day she looked at me and said, "Hey, watch me do my exercises." She stood up and shook her butt around like she had a bug in her underwear. Another day I walked up, and she said, "Sit down, you old heifer," with that same mischievous twinkle in her eye. We called each other "old heifers" every time we saw each other after that.

She told me the most ridiculous stories about being old. She said one day while on the porch alone she got warm and peeled off her sweater to just wear her pink T-shirt she had on underneath. She didn't realize she actually took the T-shirt off with the sweater, and she sat topless in her rocking chair for an hour waving at passersby like usual before she realized she was half naked. She laughed so hard when she told me this story and just shrugged her shoulders as if saying oh well. Sometimes you find yourself topless on the porch. That's life.

And then, on one boring, regular weekday afternoon, she stopped rocking and looked at me and said, "You know what? You are my best friend, and you are my family."

Edna had no idea that like her, I was essentially all alone in Memphis. Yes, I had my wonderful, amazing husband, but he was working long hours, and me being depressed and going home to a dark, lonely old house was hard. My family was thousands of miles away, and I had yet to make many friends or any sort of reliable community. I felt very alone, except when I was sitting next to my fellow heifer. Just me and Edna, on that porch, rocking as the Memphis sun began to set, evening after evening. In those moments I had somebody, and she had somebody, and I think that meant something to us both.

So I told her she was my best friend too. And my family. And I genuinely meant it. I loved that woman, and she helped me keep my head above the water as I pulled out of depression and set down roots in our new city.

The years passed, and we remained close. On her birthday every April I would bring her a little slice of cake from Otherlands Coffee Bar around the corner and pick her up a six-pack of Ensure from the grocery store. She always tried to make me drink them with her. Hard pass, Edna. She had such a strong will to keep living, even as she approached her upper nineties. "I might give out but I won't give up," she would say. "I just want to see what will happen to me tomorrow!"

The Tennessee seasons changed year after year, and so did life. Things got busier, I made amazing friends who were not seventy years older than me, and I moved one mile farther away from her, which in the small city of Memphis felt far. But I always made it over to see Edna and sit with her on the porch, listening to her same strong mantras over and over again. Edna continued to be medicine to my soul, and I hope I was to her as well. Together, the ultimate odd couple with decades between us, we would rock in those chairs, taking life one day at a time, just doing the best we could.

If that isn't the ultimate life lesson, I don't know what is. That we just need to take it one day at a time and do the best we can, no matter what is thrown at us. Death, heartache, singleness, depression, money issues, loneliness, whatever. If Edna could focus on those two things to help keep her head above water, despite all she had been through, I think I could too. Also, I need to buy my own rocking chair ASAP. That feels important for a life well contemplated and well lived.

CHAPTER SIXTEEN

FREE YOURSELF FROM THE SHAME AROUND MENTAL HEALTH. BECAUSE WHO HAS THE TIME FOR SHAME ANYMORE

There is still a lot of stigma around mental illness, unfortunately. Even with all the internet positivity, awareness months, and people beginning to open up about their suffering—which are all wonderful steps—we still have a ways to go in society to be more empathetic and understanding of people who are struggling in this way. Myself included.

See, I have a stigma against my *own* mental illness, which is pretty ridiculous. Even writing the words "mental illness" makes me feel uncomfortable. It's not *that*, not for me. I don't have a mental illness, nah. I just get deeply sad where it hurts to exist or panic like an asthmatic ape in times of great stress.

But despite how much I appreciate when others are open and honest about their struggles, I have had trouble admitting I have anxiety and depression. Which just seems silly. This is a real thing.

Denying isn't helping me, you, or the person reading this who is silently suffering and full of shame and embarrassment and confusion over why they can't just "get it together" like everyone else appears to do on the internet. (Lies.) Personally, I am working to fight against my own self-imposed stigma in a way that is right for me. I think in situations like this, where you are trying to just manage your junk the best way possible, that is all you can do. Do what is best for you, and be kind to others along the way.

In working to fight for my health and bust through my old, creaky personal stigmas, I do a few things. I remain open about my struggles with my circle of friends, with my family, and in my writing. I don't dwell on it or get dramatic about it, but if I am having a bad mental health day or can tell I am slipping below the surface, I tell my people. I tell my friends or Kyle, and they simply pray and listen, and it helps. And then I do everything I can to get my head above water again quickly, whether that be get some rest, exercise, change what I eat, or remember to take my medicine.

For me it's important to be honest and open about when I'm struggling because during the times when I was hyperventilating and in so much internal pain from a panic attack I felt my soul explode or my skin hurt from the amount of depression weighing down on me, I would tell myself these lies: *I am the only one. I am the only one who can't hold it all together. Nobody else gets this nutso. What if someone saw you like this? What is wrong with you? I am the only one.*

What kind of messed up internal trash talk is THAT? But when I hear or read about someone else being raw and upfront about their mental health struggles, I breathe a huge sigh of relief. Every time I am reminded it isn't just me gives me the life-giving strength to keep walking through the dark days and work toward a stronger, more stable, and truthful version of myself.

I once heard a powerful testimony of a girl who had severe onset depression during her third pregnancy and had to step away from her other two children and go receive longer, inpatient care. And when I heard that, you know what went through my mind? Not judgments. I didn't "tsk tsk" at her like cranky Aunt Karen. Instead my heart was filled with compassion for what she walked through and the strength that must have taken to not only endure that hard season but then use it to speak to other women and inspire them.

I also thought, *I get it.* I get how she could get that low where she had to make the extremely difficult decision to step away from her two other little babies for a few weeks and get the help she needed. And I was so grateful she shared that story, which I know must have been so challenging for her to do. But I needed to hear about her dark days, then her strength and triumph as she stepped back into the light, and I am sure other women listening that day did too. And I realized if I can have compassion and empathy for her and her story, I certainly should try to do the same for myself.

Being reminded that it isn't just me who has low moments is life giving. I need all the reminders, folks. And if you are struggling with mental health right now, here is a loving piece of written proof it isn't just you either. It can feel so isolating, so hopeless, but it isn't. Next time you are lying face down in the kitchen crying into your unwashed floor, I am right there with ya, sister. Been there, done that, cried on that floor. Used my tears to then wash it. You are not alone.

My bout of depression in Memphis was a doozy. Quite simply, it hurt to exist, and doing any tiny task took about ten times the strength and effort. I was exhausted by simply trying to function. It was pretty dang awful and scary, but mostly it just annoyed me—and my upstairs apartment neighbor who could hear me weeping.

It annoyed me because I was in that place *again*. I was so tired of being depressed. I was so tired of stupid panic attacks. I was so tired of having to deal with it once more and making poor Kyle have to deal with it. I wanted it gone from my life for good. I never again wanted to wake up with a chest tight with dread before my feet even hit the floor for the day. Instead, I wanted to wake up every morning and feel like a glittery Richard Simmons on a good hair day during his bestselling workout video wearing his best leotard. That is the level of life goals I aspire to. Instead, I just felt like the version of Richard Simmons who has hidden from society so long someone felt compelled to make a podcast about it.[1] And I was mad about that.

But not only was I so sick of being depressed and having panic attacks over extremely stressful situations—like the one time at the grocery store when Kyle decided to walk the opposite direction around the store as we normally did[2]—I was also simply getting older. I was growing up, yo. And by the grace of God I had a little bit more fire under my butt to take care of business like a grown woman. I was ready to fight extra hard to get a handle on my mental health. I knew it would likely always be something I struggle with, but I was determined to remain one step ahead of it. And truthfully, part of that fire was fueled by my

---

[1] It is called *Missing Richard Simmons*. So good. I give it 10/10 glittery leotards. Highly recommended.

[2] That really happened. Diagnose that, psychiatrist! Looking back it's kind of funny but also shows me how sick I was. But also, Kyle, when we get to the grocery store, we go to the right, not the left, okay? Never to the left.

desire to be a mom. I wanted to have better mental health because I was ready to mom it up, join the club, and jump into the minivan gang.[3] But even with our tiny Toyota, Kyle and I were ready to start the whole "becoming parents process," and I realized having a child was going to be a very mentally taxing journey, and I should probably enter that from the healthiest place possible. But more so, I wanted whatever precious human being we brought into the world to have the best version of myself to take care of them. I think kids deserve that. So I was ready to fight the good fight to get my mental health under control once and for all, for myself and for my future baby.

So a few things had to happen. First, I had to fully accept and realize fighting against depression and anxiety may be a part of me forever. This wasn't just "something that happened to me once in Austin." Falling into a pretty bad spot had happened multiple times since then and may again in the future, dang it. Denying that this is simply a part of my genetic makeup wasn't going to help me, anything, or anyone, so I decided to throw that habit out the window like a Big Mac wrapper on a highway in 1980 when people still did weird things like that.

For a long time my struggles with depression and panic attacks were something only Kyle and I knew about, and that made it feel extra heavy and dark to me. Plus, I don't think it was healthy for him to be the only one in my life who was aware of what I was dealing with. That's a lot to carry on your own. Taking the veil off my "secret" that really shouldn't have been all that secretive was freeing. Making it less of a big thing, well, made it less of a big thing. And I think that is a good step in the right direction.

---

[3]Just kidding—I am forever on team no minivan, though I guess I do understand their appeal. But nah bro.

On a whole other playing field, I had to get rid of Christian guilt around being depressed or anxious, and especially about having to take medicine. For some reason, there is this extra level of stigma around mental health issues in some Christian circles. For example, someone in Austin I knew refused to take medicine, even though a doctor prescribed it for her and she was greatly struggling, because she said she wanted God to heal her. And that's fine, I supposed, but I saw her deeply hurting for years. It scared me. I was worried for her. And her saying that God would just heal her without meds made me feel a bit guilty about my own use of medicine, even though I knew at a rational level it was helping me so very much. And I one thousand percent do believe God can heal in miraculous ways, but perhaps sometimes that comes in the form of an SSRI. In the words of Glennon Doyle, "Jesus loves me this I know, for he gave me Lexapro." For me, what I was experiencing wasn't something I could just "pray away," but bless your little hearts for suggesting it. Do I believe God can fully heal me? Yes! But will healing come in the form of medicine? So far, that answer is yes. And that's not just a lack of faith. It's simply a lack of serotonin levels in my brain . . . so, there ya go.

I don't know why people have mental health problems. I also don't know why people get irritable bowel syndrome. But what I *do* know is they are both just physical illnesses that happen in your body and are usually just a product of your genes. Or jeans, if you wear them too tight and it starts to get to you. And nobody ever says if you poop weird you must be less of a Christian. Nobody shames you for not just trying to pray away your uncomfortable gas situation. The same should be true for mental health issues.

Being open about my struggles with my family and God helped. Being on my medicine helped. But it didn't help completely. So I kept fighting, and I kept trying things to get myself to a place where I felt strong and stable. And by "things," I obviously mean any woo woo, hippie, natural solution or suggestion I came across online. Because the internet knows all, right?

Here are a few holistic things I have tried over the years to improve my mental and physical health that I feel need an honorable mention in this chapter. Mostly just to make fun of them a bit. Because while I am all about natural and holistic methods— I have found a lot of help from alternative medicine and more natural methods of doing things—there is also just a huge side of that which is trying to make money off of people who are desperate to feel better. So I take all natural healing solutions with a grain of salt now. Himalayan sea salt, to be exact, as apparently it is a magical crystal from space. Let's actually start with that . . .

Salt lamps. Apparently these pink-colored rock lights are supposed to suck up negative ions and help boost your serotonin. Like, what the literal heck. They are made from Himalayan sea salt, which you can also sprinkle on your french fries if you want, which is very confusing. How can a lamp also be made out of a seasoning? What's next, a chili powder pendant light? Salt lamps have proven themselves to be not much more than a solidified lava lamp on my night stand, not a magical healing genie. While I do appreciate the sunset hue they give off, it basically ends at that. A sunset-colored lamp that also looks like it could have been something E.T. brought down with him from his ship. But bless it for trying to heal all the world's illnesses. Just keep lighting up that drab corner of my bedroom and making my food taste delicious, and I think that is good enough for me.

Essential oils. Do you guys want to join my Young Living team? A startup kit only costs $39,392.24, and this month only you get an extra bottle of Thieves Cleaner if you recruit ninety more people over a three-day period. Just kidding. I will never join a team of any sort, unless it involves kickball and happy hour afterward. Listen, I know a lot of people will be miffed by this but hear me: I do love essential oils. A lot actually! I use them almost every day. Headache? Peppermint. Feeling sad? You better sprinkle on that orange oil, girl. The thing is, I am cheap and have ended up just buying the discount ones on Amazon. I am sure there are people reading this who are currently inhaling ninety gallons of lavender oil to calm their feelings of horror over reading this fact, but sorry. The oils I get still do the job they need to for me! Lavender helps me relax, lemon makes my home smell great while we are cleaning up, frankincense clears up mysterious skin issues on my face, and of course Thieves calms my worries about getting sick. Except mine is actually called Theifs because, well, it is an Amazon off-brand. I just get a little tired of seeing people post about their oily ways online. I mean, I just want to see funny memes and baby pictures, not about how Kimberly from Ohio is now at a triple diamond status. But oils do smell good, so they have that going for them. And lavender does help me to relax some, but that's about where the magic of it all ended for me. Joining a multi-level marketing scheme is not the cure for mental illness. Perhaps the opposite. But essential oils can make your home smell like Christmas year round, so I guess we shouldn't write them off completely.

St. John's wort and other herbal supplements. Who is St. John, and why am I ingesting his disgusting skin growth? These are the questions I would ask myself as I took these supplements, which allegedly were supposed to boost my mood. This was just one of the herbal remedies I tried to help encourage my brain to behave like a lady should, instead of an angry and sad youth on a Rumspringa gone sour. Some herbs really did help to various degrees—valerian root definitely helped with sleep and if you have the Sunday Scaries. The downside is it smells like an old donkey's butt, but if you can look past that, you are on your way to a restful, calm night. Ginkgo does help me focus almost as much as my college friends who would take one too many of their Adderall pills. Actually not nearly that much, but enough! But I knew there was no amount of herb that was going to fully fix my little struggling mass of gray matter. For me, complete healing could not be found in the vitamin aisle of the grocery store—just behind the counter at CVS from a person in a lab coat.

Also, I just googled *wort* versus *wart* because spelling is difficult, and I learned *wort* means juice of a plant. *Wart* means crusty growth thing on a witch's nose. The more you know. *Cue NBC's 1990s-sounding theme music.*

Oil pulling. Well, well, well, what can I say about this disgusting holistic trend except that it is GROSS. Looking back, I can't believe I even tried this. What you do is put a big ol' goop of oil in your mouth—coconut was my oil of choice, but feel free to do olive or anything else, I suppose, just short of motor—and swish it around like it's Listerine. The "pulling" means you are supposed to pull it back and forth between your teeth in an aggressive swish, swish manner like you are trying to floss with a big blob of warm, greasy goop. How in the world would this help with depression? Don't know, but the Interwebs told me it would, so swish, swish I went! I tried it, it did nothing, and now I want to gag even thinking about it. Don't try this, people. Greasy teeth are not the cure for your mental or physical ailments. In fact, they may cause more ailments if you actually drool and then slip on your greasy spit, fall, and injure yourself in a puddle of shame.

Probiotics. For some reason, probiotics are supposed to be the ultimate healer in life. And yes, I am sure they are good, on some strange gut level that I don't fully understand. But anytime I took them they did nothing for me except empty my bank account because they cost so much money. But after trying them and not getting the hype, I would be like, *Oh, maybe I just need more expensive probiotics.* So I would up my game to more "billions of bacteria per pill," and it made no difference. So then, the woo woo marketers would get to me even more. Obviously a dried pill on a shelf contains dead bacteria—you need ones that are still alive and refrigerated! So, I would go to the fridge section of the Whole Foods supplement aisle and try my luck with those. I noticed nothing. As a last-ditch effort, I went back to Whole Foods and asked the lingering worker, likely named Sage, what she recommends, and when she pointed me to the *most* expensive kind of probiotics, I thought, *Oh, those should work, right?* No. Sage was wrong. I was wrong. Everything is wrong. And now I am broke. I am sure these little pills full of "good germs" help with something in the human body. Digestion? Bloat? I don't know. Ask Sage. But as for mental health, they just didn't give me the fix I was hoping for.

The point of all the hoopla is this: sometimes, you need real help, beyond what the pretty natural health Instagram ads are chucking at you. Yes, some trendy hippie things you find online can do some good, and that's only a positive thing. But it's okay if it isn't enough. It's okay if taking a nice walk every morning and slathering on so many essential oils that you smell like your Aunt Bertha put her potpourri dish in a blender isn't cutting it. It is okay if you can't find the fix you need in the aisles at Whole Foods, or even just the church pews. I am there with you. I need the extra help and am here, shame free, admitting that and inviting anyone who needs to join me.

So in Memphis, as I was working on my mental health and wasting my money on all the hippie dippy things I could muster up in a Google search, I realized there was one thing I hadn't tried yet that I may need to. Partially because I am cheap and it is expensive but also because it was another one of those things I didn't want to admit I needed. Therapy. I needed therapy. Like bad. And probably pretty dang quick, since I was working toward the end game of being a mom in the near future. This was about my mental health, yes, but also about working toward raising a family in as much of a stable, healthy environment as I possibly could, and there were some major roadblocks in my way. So I decided to get help.

CHAPTER SEVENTEEN

IT IS OKAY TO SEE A THERAPIST. BONUS POINTS IF YOUR THERAPIST MAY BE A MAGICAL ANCIENT WIZARD

found a therapist online and made an appointment. As I sat on the little leather couch in her waiting room, I could hear every word of the patient who was in there before me. *Great, we're off to a good start,* I thought. I reminded myself to talk quietly when I got in there, but we all know that is impossible for me. Cool. I was about to tell a complete stranger all my deepest darkest secrets, and then as a bonus I would also be telling the person who would be waiting to go in after me. I am sure there would be some level of awkward eye contact made as we walked past each other in the lobby.

When it was time for my appointment, she opened the door and let the previous patient out and then welcomed me in. Instantly I saw she wasn't a therapist but actually more resembled an ancient wizard with a foggy, magical eye. That is what she looked like at least. Old, tiny, stoic and with this blasted eye that looked like it had a thunderstorm currently raging away on her cornea. That eye, I was sure, was going to peer right into my soul, and then a laser was going to squirt out of it and heal all my problems. That eyeball, this lady, was clearly magic.

To put it less dramatically, she was in her eighties and had glaucoma, but there was something about her foggy eye and instant calming presence that gave me a sense of peace and mystery. And I think that is a good way to start a therapy session, right? With a little mystery.

I sat down and she began asking all the normal first session questions. I told her about my family, about my million cross-country moves, about my dear beloved Kyle, and about how I kept having bouts of depression and panic attacks, and I was ready to kick all that ish to the curb. It was all pretty basic, straightforward therapy stuff, until she asked one more question.

"Okay, that is about it for today," she said, as our hour had flown by. Clearly all normal sense of time is erased when in her magical presence. "Anything else you would like to add?" Dr. Magic Wizard asked.

I paused, knowing I was about to get really weird and drop an emotional bomb at the very last second of our session. It was a really big bomb, and one I didn't want to drop, because I knew it would hurt. I would rather just pretend the bomb didn't exist at all and carry the heavy sucker around for the rest of my life. But deep in my soul I knew I needed to because I had been avoiding dealing with this large, very traumatic issue for about, oh, the past decade or so, and clearly that wasn't working well for me and my brain anymore. I knew it was time to process through some pain. Ugh. Can't we just binge a crime show on Netflix instead to distract ourselves from our own inner turmoil with someone else's?

"Ah, yes actually," I said. "My best friend died in a car crash when I was nineteen, and I think about it every single day and it still hurts all the time and I am pretty sure it is the cause of a lot of my mental health problems." I instantly started crying, just to really lay the awkwardness on thick for her.

How is that for an exciting therapy session plot twist, wizard lady? Just trying to keep ya on your magical toes.

"Oh," Dr. Magic Wizard said, looking genuinely surprised. "Thank you for telling me that," she said softly, which I felt was a nice thing to say. I liked this woman. I decided I would return.

We wrapped it up, and I biked home, tears still streaming down my face. I knew the time had come—a decade later—to try and process the death of my friend. But I didn't want to. I was scared to. I was just trying to avoid pain, always, at any cost. But everything in my body was telling me, "Katie. Deal with this now, or we are only going to get sicker."

A week later at the next session, Dr. Wiz started by asking me to tell her every single detail about my friend and the day she died. Nobody had ever asked me that before, and I thought it was a weird question. But as I walked through it all, it made it all feel validated and real, not like some fake trauma I invented. It was real, and she was helping me acknowledge that.

"Well, her name was Jenna," I began. And then I jumped right in.

Jenna and I met freshman year of college, and she instantly became my person at school. It was me and her, all day every day. We did everything together—ate every meal, hung out every night and every weekend. We visited each other's families on holidays together and took the most amazing and ridiculous, classic, college kid spring break road trip all over Florida in her grandma's minivan. I had never been so close to someone as I was to her (besides Kyle of course). We fit together so easily, and I had never felt so unconditionally loved by a friend and so bonded in such a short amount of time. But that is what college does—it ties you so close with people you just met who are in the exact same phase of life as you. We were away from our families and our childhood best friends, so we became both of those for each other.

Around Jenna I felt I could be my total weird self, and I loved everything about how weird she was right back. She had strawberry blond hair, loved the color orange, and painted the most gorgeous watercolors. She loved bean dip and French culture and told me once she wanted to be a missionary doctor overseas one day. She got straight As in college but also taught me how to play beer pong and what the term *party foul* meant. She was from New Jersey, so these things were basically part of her heritage. Her faith in the Lord was so, so beautiful. She never judged anyone, no matter what quirks they brought to the table. She loved people so fully and radically, and she was the most literal example of Jesus walking on earth I had ever seen. And I mean that. We were both equal parts wild hippies and total school nerds. We would share a giant towel at the beach and she would whip out her iPod.[1] We would each take an ear bud and she would play me all of her favorites, which quickly became mine—mostly every single song by the band Brand New, which I still blare all the time when I just want to feel not like a creaky old adult person. The night before she turned eighteen, we ran through the streets together singing their song "Soco Amaretto Lime" at the top of our lungs in the salty Florida air.

---

[1] Remember iPods? Those were the days.

I'm gonna stay eighteen forever
So we can stay like this forever

We did everything and nothing together, but no matter what it was, if it was her and me, it was fun. One night we went line dancing with a bunch of friends—because that makes sense in South Florida, right? We didn't feel like going home after we were done, so we went to the gas station and each bought our own two liters of Diet Mountain Dew (gross) and drank that aspartame-soaked caffeine right from the giant bottles as we drove all over West Palm Beach, windows down, music blaring, our hair, still salty from being in the ocean earlier that morning, whipping around us as we laughed and just enjoyed being *young*. We snuck behind a Krispy Kreme and snagged a giant bag of discarded donuts, and I taught her the art of "donutting someone." Which basically means we drove by our friends' lawns and balconies and tossed a bunch of donuts at them, just because we were weird like that. We ended the night by jumping in the pool of our friends' apartment complex before driving back to campus soaking wet with a giant half-empty bag of donuts in her back seat, singing, laughing, and enjoying life in the sweet, pure way you can at that time.

Our last night together before she was set to drive home for the summer, we hung out until three in the morning, visiting friends, driving, listening to her music, and doing errands that needed to be done. She would head to New Jersey the next day, and I would head to Minnesota the next week. We both talked about how we were going to miss each other so much, but also how excited we were to come back to Florida in the fall and be roommates. Jenna had gathered up some of our favorite friends and applied to live in this new "themed housing" complex. For a conservative Christian school, this was just their watered-down version of a sorority house. Yes, it was a former homeless shelter they now put college students in, but we were essentially going to live in an apartment complex with no RA and a bunch of other people. It was the most unsupervised yet still on-campus option possible, and we felt we hit the lottery. Since you had to have a theme to apply, ours was "God's Great Outdoors." We said in our application that sometimes we would clean the beach, or something like that. Nature and stuff. They loved it, and we quickly made a decision to change our name to the "Nature Hut." Oh, to be young and live somewhere called the Nature Hut with your best friends.

We were excited for that. And for another adventure-filled year at our college we loved so much, for more beach trips and nights spent just hanging out and laughing.

Before we said goodbye, we gave each other a massive bear hug, and I can still remember what that hug felt like to this day. I forget a lot of things, but when things happen that you don't even know are significant at the time, they get ingrained in your mind more deeply than most other memories.

Jenna had taught me so much that year about what true, genuine friendship was. And about how to love people better, and more like Jesus did. She taught me how to break down my legalistic Lutheran upbringing and learn more about the unconditional, wild, ruthless love of Christ. And she did that just by living her life *well*. And loving people *well*. It wasn't by anything she said but what she did. I was so blessed to be the one right by her side during one of the best years of a young person's life—that first year of college, of independence, and of figuring out who you are and who you want to become. And, it turned out, the last year of her time on earth, and I don't take that privilege lightly.

The morning after our goodbye bear hug, I woke up to a text from her. She said she was on the road and she loved me so much. She was heading home in the same minivan we had driven all over the state just a few months prior, bouncing from beach town to beach town and reveling in our new independence.

A few hours later, I got the call. The kind of call that stops the world from spinning, takes the breath from your lungs, and changes your life forever. Jenna was gone. Her car was hit by a truck, and that was that. My sweet, precious friend was simply gone.

After Jenna died, my heart shattered in a way nobody should ever have to feel. What was even more confusing for me is that I was so young—barely nineteen. And I had just spent the most perfect, amazing, soul-nourishing freshman year at this gorgeous college where most everyone there loved Jesus. My faith grew, my love for God grew, I grew. And then just like that, it was all ripped into a million pieces. That was confusing for me then, and is still now.

So instead of goofing around in the Nature Hut with Jenna like we had planned, my sophomore year was full of weeping in church bathroom stalls in the middle of a service, or nights trying to numb my pain if only for a moment by doing dumb stuff like drinking 99 Bananas in a parking lot with my friends.[2] Because when you are twenty and your soul is shattered, life still moves forward with classes and jobs and the thousands of other non-grieving people on campus around you. Everything propels

---

[2] I am pretty sure we are the only people in the history of the universe to ever actually purchase 99 Bananas, before that night and after. It tasted like you set an old, spotty brown banana on fire with jet fuel and then swallowed it. So awful.

forward and it is confusing, and I don't think I took a moment to process my pain in a healthy way.

Somehow I made it through that year and the rest of college. Kyle and I got engaged and then married after junior year, and we were thinking of grad school and moving and then moving again. Those years were full of so much distraction. We were always looking ahead to the next thing; it was easy not to look back. But every single day, I would think of my friend and have a heaviness on my heart. When I met new friends, I always wondered if we would grow as close as Jenna and I did, then felt hurt all over again when we didn't. During a hard time in New York, I would walk the streets and play her favorite music loudly and almost pretend she was there with me. Which sounds nice, in a way, but I knew it wasn't healthy. How I dealt with her death wasn't healthy for me. Clearly the wounds had yet to heal up at all, and they were starting to fester.[3]

When I was looking for a therapist, I knew I didn't want one who was Christian based. Which may seem strange, but after Jenna died, I heard way too many hurtful "Christian" sayings at my university that, while well intentioned, hurt me, and most were not even theologically sound. *Christianese*, as it has been dubbed. During that time, if one more person told me that Jenna dying "happened for a reason," I was pretty sure I would karate kick them in the gullet.

As I processed my hurt, my simple theology was being held to the fire. I had to walk through whether I believed everything I had learned about God up to that point, and if I was willing to continue to believe it even after a tragedy that shattered my life and sense of safety. And in that time, it was refreshing to have all the well-meaning

---

[3] *Fester* is the most disgusting word of all time. So glad I could include it in this very serious chapter.

but frustrating cliché Christian sayings off the table so I could take a hard look at what was really happening in my brain and body after I experienced this trauma, and when that was at a healthier spot, I could attempt to reconcile what happened within my faith.

After that second session when Dr. Magic Wizard made me go deep into details I didn't want to remember, I swore as I biked home I was not going to go back. And I just swore. She ripped some pretty nasty bandages off of very old, unhealed wounds, and that hurt. But I did go back. Again and again I returned, and slowly, it began to hurt a little bit less. Things I didn't even realize were weighing me down so heavily felt a little bit lighter. Slowly and with kind grace, Dr. Magic Wizard pointed out the strength it took for me to get through such an awful tragedy. And if I got through it before, I could get through basically anything else. And that freed a lot in me. She taught me you can't worry yourself into safety. Worrying doesn't give you control over anything. It just sucks up energy. Having extreme anxiety over whether something was going to happen to Kyle didn't make him any more safe. I needed to hear that.

Dr. Magic Wizard taught me that yes, life is uncertain and we don't know what will happen, but there is one thing I can count on: my own strength. I made it through Jenna's death, and I could make it through anything else if I had to.

Slowly, in Dr. Magic Wizard's office, with her glittery oracle eyeball, she peeled off layers of old, sticky pain and finally helped me to get my head above water—something I had been unable to do on my own. She also told me to stay on my medicine forever and to never move across the country again unless it was somewhere with family nearby. And hey, the lady wasn't wrong. She gave me tools I didn't know I needed or even know existed, tools I still use to this day when I can feel myself slipping into a bad place mentally.

A few years after Jenna died, I was driving to a memorial painting party with her childhood best friend, Lauren, who I am now very close with. We both did not want to go to the event, as it brought up a lot of pain. But as we were driving on the dark New Jersey backroads, we were talking about all the dumb stuff people said to us after we lost our sweet friend. I told her I hated when people would say "everything happens for a reason" because I can't see one single thing that makes what happened "okay." I had spent so much time and mental energy after Jenna died trying to find the "thing" that would justify it—for the glory of God, whatever. But I didn't see anything in front of me that felt like a fair trade for the pain not only I felt but also her parents, family, and everyone who loved her and didn't have her in their life anymore felt.

Lauren agreed, and then said something that freed so much in me: "Katie, I totally believe God works all things together for a greater purpose," she said. "But sometimes we won't ever know what that purpose is on this side of heaven. That was never promised to us. And that is okay."

Dang. She was so right. There is no promise in Scripture that we will ever know all the whys behind hard things that happen in our life. What we are promised is that God is alive and working, and he cares about every single hair on our head and all of our pain. When Lauren reminded me of this and gave me permission to stop looking for some mysterious reason for my pain and just rest in the daily love that God surrounds me with, I felt I could finally exhale.

I no longer think about why Jenna died; instead I focus on the miracles of goodness that have happened after such a deep hurt. Like the simple miracle that my heart could again feel joy, even after being smashed into a million bits. That anyone who loved someone as special as Jenna could go on to find joy, new life, new beginnings after she was taken from us is simply a miracle, and only happened through God's grace. I may not understand why everything happens, but I do know that God will yet again fill our mouths with laughter and our hearts with songs of joy.[4] That is a promise from God found right in Scripture, not a cheesy Christian cliché you find on a barn-chic sign at Hobby Lobby. That is truth. God can bring us to a place of laughter again, no matter how far from that we are taken. God can heal all hearts and can bring sunshine even after the worst of storms. And to me, that is one of the most beautiful things I have ever seen. Hard, yet beautiful.

I kept going to Dr. Magic Wizard, and the amount of healing and stability she helped me accomplish was worth every penny. One day she graduated me, quite unexpectedly!

"I think you are ready to move on, there is not much more work we need to do here," she said, her special eye twinkling a bit brighter. I was surprised but happy I guess, my brain being given some sort of gold star of recognition.

A few weeks later, the thought suddenly came to me and I gasped: she was probably just ready to die! I mean, she was really, really old. Think of the damage a therapist would cause to her already sensitive patients if she up and croaked! I see you, Dr. Wiz. I see your ways and how you were trying to spare us all one more sorrow. Respect. But then I googled her, and she is still kicking it. I guess I really was ready to move on and free up more time and space for others to enter into her magical midst, stare into that sparkling mystical eye, and heal.

---

[4]Job 8:21. Look, this is another normal footnote, not a weird, funny random one! Anyway, the point is, the verse is Job 8:21.

PART SEVEN

GROWING A HUMAN BEING

Hey there. Having kids is straight CRAZY. Not in the "oh man, I just got pooped on in the middle of Target this is so nuts" type of way. Sure, that is weird, whatever. But I'm talking about the sheer amount of physical and emotional strength it takes to create a human, birth them, and then keep them alive for the rest of your life. Literally astronomical. Yet oddly so worth it. It makes zero sense. You may not be at a place where kids are on your radar, you may be yearning for a little human more than anything else, or you may prefer to snuggle cats the rest of your life. Whatever your journey, this part will focus on this one truth: you can do the hard things. You can. You are stronger than you know. Way stronger, actually.

Having kids has taught me that far more than I could have predicted or imagined. It *forced* me to get stronger. Nothing—not even an obnoxiously loud CrossFit trainer—could have launched me into this level of inner strength. Being pregnant, birthing, and then caring for babies has shown me more than anything else in my life how deep our inner strength goes. On the days when you are straight-up tapped out of that strength, because that definitely will happen, that is the moment God can show up. He shows up, fills you up, and gets you up and moving forward. And it is truly a miracle.

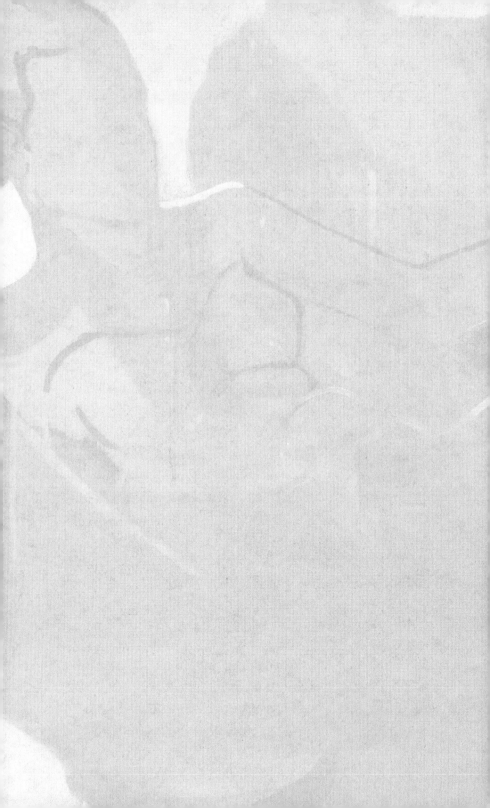

CHAPTER EIGHTEEN

SOMETIMES YOU TRY TO GROW A BABY BUT GROW A MUSTACHE INSTEAD

Life, no matter how hard you fight to contain it, is out of our control. That is a lesson God teaches us all pretty early on, yet it can take a bit longer for some to accept that than others. (Me. I am the one who has a hard time accepting that.)

A major way this lesson is revealed is through the process of starting a family. Trying to get pregnant may actually be the most extreme example of how some things, no matter how hard you try, pray, or wish for them, are completely out of your hands. For many, the journey from childless couple to parents buying jumbo packs of Pampers at Walmart at 9:00 p.m. on a Friday night is a long, challenging process full of tears, procedures, crushed dreams, and long seasons of waiting. For others, they may not even have kids on their radar, but they look at each other in a certain way then find themselves with a baby ten months later. With something as miraculous and sacred as a new human life, it makes sense it isn't something easily accomplished, as with most beautiful things in this world. Kyle and I learned trying to add a baby to our family was not going to be as hastily achieved as when we got our cats from the humane society. Here is $50. Thank you for my cats. Goodbye. While I wish everything in life was that easy and resulted in that many kitten cuddles, it isn't the case.

We were feeling settled into Memphis, our life and routines, and decided now felt like a good time to try and start a family. And by "now feels like a good time," I really mean we kinda sorta thought that this was the time God was calling us to move into this next phase of life, but who is to really say? I don't think there is ever a "perfect" time to try and get pregnant, or actually anything that involves moving into a big, new scary situation with no guaranteed outcomes. And while those large life changes often turn out to be great, jumping from the high dive can prove to be a bit unsettling, no matter how you launch off. You just have to take the leap and trust God is with you as you flail your way to the surface.

Kyle and I were optimistic and excited to become parents. We both loved working and our life together but knew having kids was something we both wanted. So we began to try. I'll spare you the specific details, you creep. That month, the very first day you are told you can take a pregnancy test, I did, all by myself while Kyle was at work. I looked down at the little pee stick, and there it was—the faintest line, but a line nonetheless.

I thought about how I wanted to tell Kyle the news. I am not that Pinteresty and creative when it comes to these things. But I did once see the idea of putting a bun in the oven, then telling your spouse to check said oven and watch to see how long it takes him to figure it out. That is about the highest level of creativity I felt comfortable with. So I went to CVS and bought a Honey Bun—the first and last time I will ever make this purchase. Why not announce your pregnancy with the most disgusting (yet likely delicious) processed food item possible from your dingy CVS on the corner, right? Off to a good start with this parenting thing.

I put the bun in the oven, and when Kyle got home, I told him to go see what was in there. He opened it and got it almost instantly. Of course he was thrilled, and I was thrilled that he got my bun pun.

We FaceTimed my family right away and went about trying to find an ob-gyn and making our first appointment. Still being newish to Memphis and not having a ton of friends who I felt I could ask for the name of their hoo-ha doctor, I was just guessing at who to go with.[1]

Until our appointment, Kyle and I talked endlessly about potential names, due dates, and what kind of baby our sweet little bean was going to be. Becoming pregnant is wild because even though you don't know this person who is the size of a poppy seed, you love them so deeply almost immediately. I couldn't help but wonder about who they were, if they were a boy or girl, and what I wanted their nursery to look like. The dreams and hopes came strong and fast, and we were so excited to have a child and become a little family unit.

At our first visit, I liked our doctor's shoes, so I decided sure, she can deliver my child, why not. She didn't smile much, and if I cracked any jokes she looked at me blankly, but that's fine, right? Bad social skills sometimes come with being a smart, highly educated, capable medical professional. At least that's what I told myself as I sat uncomfortably on the table, nervous and confused about what to expect. She eventually did a scan, and there on the

---

[1] I mean, I guess I could have asked Edna, but that could have gotten real weird real quick.

screen was our little baby, a tiny circle flickering with each beat of its microscopic heart.

Awkward Doctor scowled a bit, which was on brand for her apparently. "It is a good size, but the heartbeat is a little slow," she said. "But don't worry about it. See you in a few weeks for the next scan." Kyle and I asked the normal follow-up questions as she washed her hands and tried to leave the room, but she kept assuring us, "It's fine. This is pretty normal, don't worry about it."

The grumpy nice-shoe lady said to chillax, so that is what we tried to do. What did we know, right? We were new to this game, going in completely ignorant and just listening to whatever the doctor said. Googling told us every baby is different, the heart range fluctuates, or our child was likely a space alien. It was hard to get any straight information. So we just waited until our next appointment, trying not to think about that short yet completely loaded sentence the doctor told us. The heartbeat is a little slow. We didn't know what this meant, but we *did* know that we already loved this tiny baby with every ounce of ourselves, and any inkling that something was wrong was suddenly the most horrifying feeling we had ever felt. But "probably fine" was what we told ourselves over and over until the next week when we went back in for another scan.

This time, the heartbeat was even slower, and the size was just under normal range, so our worrying of course went into overdrive. Deep worrying, unlike anything else we have ever experienced before. We had never met this baby, but it already was a part of us, of our story, of our lives. We loved them, whoever they were. Also, I had been so sick with morning sickness and exhausted. I was eight weeks into feeling like crap, into thinking about the baby's birthday and if it would be a boy or girl, and endless discussions and plans and hopes. Eight weeks now seems like a short amount of time, but when you are walking through it, it feels like eternity. Our whole hearts, souls, and lives had been wrapped around this pregnancy for the past two months, and even the tiniest thought of losing our little bean who had become our everything was beyond awful.

The doctor had taken blood work at my first visit. After our scan with its meh results, our faces clearly full of sheer terror, she looked at me with her stoic face.

"Your blood type is B+," she said. "See, just 'be positive.'"

Ohhhhh. That's all it takes? Just a little dose of optimism and this baby would be fine? Easy peasy. Great medical advice, lady. I no longer like your shoes.

We were scheduled to come back one week later, which became the longest waiting period of my life. My stomach was churning as we entered the exam room. And this time, there was no heartbeat at all. The little flicker on the screen was now still, and I fell completely apart. Our own hearts seemed to stop in that moment, and I just sobbed on the exam table. Kyle in his own grief tried to comfort me, and the doctors told me I could use the back door to leave so I didn't have to walk past all the other pregnant women sitting out front. They ushered me out into a back alley like some sort of baby-making failure.

Even though there was no longer a heartbeat, my little babe was still hanging on inside of me. So we decided to do a D & C. As with a lot of medical stuff, there was no clear best choice to make in this situation, but after talking with friends who also experienced loss, this seemed like the least traumatic of our options. Just like everything else with this pregnancy, Kyle and I fumbled our way through, not knowing what was happening or what to expect. So when I showed up to the procedure, I was taken aback by the drama of it all. I was in a gown, strapped to an IV, and lying in a hospital bed, still half confused at what was happening or what would happen, when a nun asked if she could pray for me. She asked if it was my first pregnancy, and I said yes. The sad look she was giving me got even sadder, and that confused me at the time, but now I get it. Any loss is so, so hard. But there is something a bit magical about being pregnant for the first time. You are so full of excitement about the brand-new adventure laid out before you, and to have it suddenly snatched away feels like an extra level of cruel.

My doctor arrived and asked, "How are you doing?" What do you even say at this moment? Sitting in a bleach-smelling room I did not want to be in, with a baby no longer living inside of me, confused, without my husband, who was now instructed to wait in the lobby, and with some nun making me feel even more depressed and confused at what was happening. Well, lady, let me tell you how I am doing, pull up a seat. So I said what most people say in situations like this: "Fine," my voice weak with nerves and overwhelming sadness. Oh fine, the one-word lie that masks so many emotions.

The doctor's phone rang just then and she answered it, right there in my room. *Oh, must be some emergency baby-birthing situation she has to address,* I told myself. Because why else would you answer a phone right as you were talking to a patient in this situation. But nah, Dr. "Be Positive" was talking to someone about something she had ordered online and was being delivered that day. I heard her discussing it as she walked away and finished the call in the hall as I sat alone in my room.

They wheeled me into surgery and put me to sleep. Then I simply woke up without a baby inside of me anymore. We went home, and I sat on the couch, surprised at the tangible emptiness I felt. The soul, the life that was once right there with me, all day every day for the past two months, was noticeably gone. The sense of loss I felt is hard to understand unless you have been through it. There is nothing else like it. The hollowness in your gut. The sense of negative space where there was once such a positive. All that energy that was once multiplying and growing was no longer.

Just as I was so unprepared for what it was going to be like to be pregnant, I was even more unprepared for what it was like to lose a baby. The loss was so visceral, so deep. And it seemed the world kept spinning around us while Kyle and I tried to process our grief. I did that whole weep loudly on the bathroom floor thing I was already accustomed to. The beluga whale cries returned in full force.

But the grief would also bubble up and catch me off guard at unexpected times. The first time we drove past the hospital where I had my D & C. When I accidentally walked down the baby aisle at Target. When I went back on birth control. Or when a friend emailed me to vote for her baby to be the next Gerber model the day after I told her about our miscarriage. Those emails are annoying to get even when you are not grieving the loss of your own baby, who, for the record, I am sure would have also been of Gerber baby glamour standards.

As with all pain, time does help heal, although sometimes I wish the grief process would speed up a bit. My body, like a rusted old clock, began to creak back into rhythm. I got my period again, but it felt so different. In fact, my whole body felt different. My boobs used to plump up like Pamela Anderson's (okay, that's an exaggeration; #bcup) and would hurt so bad even walking upstairs. Now they were deflated and painless. I only got one little cramp, and I didn't get cranky or emotional, a stark difference from the hormonal demon I used to morph into. I wasn't missing PMS, clearly. Please Jesus, take PMS away from the universe. But pregnancy itself—the exhaustion, the nausea, the mood swings and hormones surging through my body—had made me feel like my body was so out of my control. Post miscarriage, it turns out, was no better. I didn't know if I would ever feel like myself again, and that was another thing for me to grieve.

But it didn't end at funky periods and extreme sadness. Because why stop there when we are having so much fun, right? I grew a mustache. That's right. A MUSTACHE.

It wasn't too noticeable I guess—I didn't exactly look like some dirty flannel-wearing Brooklyn hipster man who resembled a cross between a Civil War general and Paul Bunyan. It wasn't that ridiculous, but it was there. For a while, I even thought I was imagining things. I have never grown any hair on my face before. But then Kyle pointed it out, as kindly as one could broach the topic of the new shadow looming over one's lip. Dang it. I was not imagining it. We squinted at it in the bathroom mirror and in multiple different light sources, and made a few scientific confirmations: there weren't any hairs (which, for the record, would at least be waxable), but it looked like someone had taken black watercolor paint and drawn a slim French mustache on me while I was sleeping, and then let out a maniacal cackle and disappeared into the night.

I googled "what causes a dark upper lip on women." I learned the shadowy beast is called *melasma* and that hormone changes were the main cause. Super cool, body. Super cool. Way to kick a lady when she's down.

I tried to bleach this non-hairy facial decoration with lemon juice. It didn't work. I slathered on so much concealer I looked like Snooki circa 2006. I did a lot of poking and squinting and let out an entire album's worth of frustrated screams (now available on Spotify). I constantly asked my husband if he could see it, and he would say "Nah" but still had this sympathetic "I am lying" look that clearly meant "Yeah bro, you got a stache."

I found I was in one of those annoying life situations where there was no way to fix the problem. So I did the next best thing: I tried to fix my attitude. Ugh. I know, it sounds like something you would learn in first grade Sunday school. But after months of grieving, weeping, and having my body and emotions spin so far out of my control, I finally surrendered to trying to make the best of my situation. This act was either out of newly acquired strength or sheer exhaustion, I am not completely sure which, but it seemed to be my only option. I had to find a way to stop crying. Especially in public at Target, because that was getting weird.

So I held on to some semblance of hope my hormones would even out and the stache would fade. Then, I defaulted to my favorite way to make really crappy situations better: I made jokes about it. I told Kyle to just start calling me the Magnificent Mustachio Woman, and he would announce me like a circus sideshow act while I paraded around and dramatically displayed my sideshow of an upper lip. I took a sip of his drink and said, "Don't worry, I didn't get any mustache in your glass." I texted him the mustache man emoji and called it my new selfie. We laughed at our pain, because sometimes, when the hurt is laying on thick and there is no way out from the blanket of suffering, you just have to crack a few jokes, if only to give yourself tiny bright spots in a hard day. Together Kyle and I tried to laugh through the hurt as much as we could, until our souls healed a bit and we felt we could strongly stand upright again.

Losing our first baby brought about a new sense of grief we had to process together unlike anything else. Yes, we had both lost loved ones before, but something about this collective grief over a child, someone who was supposed to be a part of our future, our life together, was different. But we did our best giving each other grace as we navigated these crappy waters together, until the pain of them slowly receded. I trusted one day, somehow, our baby-making journey would work out. I *had* to trust—letting my mind dip too far into the "will this ever happen for us?" territory was a dangerous place to go, though a valid fear I could feel lingering in the back of my mind. But that is where I kept it, banished to the back with my fear of an alien attack, both set aside in the dusty corner until something valid brought them out, like infertility or a UFO hovering over my home.

Until I saw another pink line on a pregnancy test, I vowed to enjoy the time of just Kyle and me and hold on to hope along the way. And make a lot of jokes to get me through everything else, including my mustached upper lip.

CHAPTER NINETEEN

YOU CAN BE A MOM
AND STILL WEAR A BIKINI.
OR NOT. YOU DO YOU, BABE

few months after our miscarriage when the doctor said we were good to go, we tried to get pregnant again.[1] We tried again, and it worked! We were yet again growing a human.

This time around, we took a blood sample the day I had my positive pregnancy test to check my hormone levels, and it showed I was low on progesterone. I had a friend tell me she once had to supplement with progesterone during her pregnancy, and she honestly felt it saved her baby. She said it was something you had to ask your doctor to check for, as they don't offer it outright, which was true. And I was so glad I did ask. With the low levels, I took supplements for the first few weeks, and they seemed to help. This new little creature stuck around, met all the heart and size ranges that were expected, and kept growing like a perfect little champion. This appeared to be the real deal—it was mom

---

[1] I of course found a new doctor. I had no desire to ever see that lady with her stupid nice shoes and terrible bedside manner ever again, telling me to just "be positive" when I was in the process of losing my child. Please know that not all doctors are jerks, so if you are seeing a doctor who is, it's okay to look elsewhere.

o'clock, folks. A few weeks in, we found out we were having a girl. I was going to have a daughter.

While pregnant, we were back home in Minnesota visiting family that summer. I was at the beach (a.k.a. the muddy lakeshore— gotta love the Midwest) with my sister, Jenny, and my nephew and niece, who were both still little babes under the age of three. Jenny was momming real hard like a total pro, which was something that overwhelmed me a bit. She seemed to have it all together, running her ship like a professional pirate on his best day, and I wondered how or if that instinct would ever come to me. But beyond her, I was looking around at all the other moms. It seemed the entire beach was infested with women who had a gaggle of tiny beasts circling their legs. It was like a mom zombie invasion, and I began to panic. This was going to be me, and being in charge of and responsible for a tiny human being was so far out of the scope of how I operated now, and I had no idea how I was ever going to make that leap from non-mom to mom without falling flat on my face in the process.

But as I sat there pregnant in the muddy sand, looking around at all the women who were boss ladying it like maternal geniuses, I saw one mom who made me even more freaked out. And it was for the most shallow reason, so please forgive me but also bear with me.

This lady was in her late twenties or early thirties, had two little ones swimming nicely in the water, and everything seemed to be peaceful and calm about her. It was all fairly normal, except for one thing. She was wearing the ugliest, frumpiest tankini of all time. I saw her and her toned legs, and her youthful, pretty face and how it contrasted against that garbage bag–resembling choice of swimwear, and I began to panic.

Will I also have to wear an ugly tankini once this baby arrives? Is that what constitutes a good mom—wearing sensible clothing and unfashionable sunglasses, responsibly slathered in sunscreen as I stand on the shores of a lake that smells like goose poop and watch my children pick up snails? IS THAT ALL I HAVE TO LOOK FORWARD TO?

Granted, my sister was right next to me and she has never owned a tankini in her life, but something about seeing that girl all decked out in her armor of classic "mom gear" scared me. Did she know something that I didn't? Because she looked like a cliché of a mom—did that mean she was a better mom? The best mom? Did her tankini hold secrets that were too lofty for my brain to ever obtain?! What knowledge was she hiding under that long, baggy swimsuit top?

I was spiraling down a dark pit of self-doubt and overwhelm. To a degree, that makes sense and is expected. I was about to have a huge change in my life—one I was *so* excited but also scared about. It is a bit strange. After you lose a baby you would think that your emotional journey during a pregnancy carried to full term should be one full of joy, gratitude, and bliss. But it isn't the case. Though I was so grateful for where I was at, I still felt all the same new-mom fears and doubts. I was also pumped full of so many hormones I had the emotional ranges of The Rock during WWE and his movie star life after—crazy to cool. The feelings were swinging pretty far and wide.

As I sat there with my tiny baby bump, I swore to myself I was never going to wear sensible tankinis. In fact, after this baby came I was pretty sure I was going to continue to wear my bikini, my questionably too-short cutoff jean shorts, and sunglasses so large and ridiculous that they would make Elton John feel jealous. That was who I was currently and had been up to this point—but how did that fit into my new role of mom? It didn't seem to line up. Could I be a mom and still be myself?

Jenny, between chasing around her babes, saw I was looking horrified on my beach towel and asked me what was up.

"I don't want to have to wear a mom tankini," I whispered as I flicked my head in the direction of the Suburban Goddess and her appropriately modest and comfortable swimwear.

Jenny looked at me like I was nuts and said, "You don't have to. You can wear whatever you want."

She was of course right, but I still worried that my personality wasn't going to be one that constituted what the world considered to be a "good mom." It wasn't about the tankini. It was deeper than that. For example, I forget things . . . a lot. I get easily distracted, and sometimes I have a panic attack because why not, right? So fun. And though I was actively working on it as I have said before, I was still kinda messy, because see above—I forget things a lot, and that includes picking up the clothes that I had placed on the floor after my shower. I think my college roommates have PTSD from my laundry pile that was always on the floor by my bed. A whole human being could have been living under that pile and we would have never known it. Will my baby get lost in my laundry pile?!

Another thing I was grappling with was working. I loved to work, and I didn't want to stop. In fact, we *needed* my income, but for some reason I still felt pressured to be a stay-at-home mom, which makes no sense. Not everyone has the privilege and option of being a full-time stay-at-home mom because ya know, money is a real thing that is needed. But even so, I felt such pressure and mom guilt about that. Like a stay-at-home mom is the only option to be fully a good mom. Welp, that wasn't going to be me, so I already felt three steps behind.

I even worried that once the baby arrived, something would change in my brain and I would *want* to stop working. I have seen it happen to so many people, and I didn't get it! Would I, too, suddenly want to stay home and just try to provide grocery money for my family through opening an Etsy shop full of cutesy baby bows? Or—God help me—would I want to become a Beachbody coach and then let the universe know about it every three minutes on social media? The *horror*. I mean, at least the second option would give me abs, but at what cost?

I was so excited to become a mom but was freaking out that in the process I wasn't going to be *me* anymore. I mean, I felt like I was already failing in terms of mom standards, and this baby wasn't even born yet. If I looked on social media, I was supposed to be taking monthly bump photos, or wearing a flowing gown in a field of flowers and delicately holding my belly as the sun set behind me and I gave my best Tyra Banks smize at the camera. I was doing nothing along those lines. If I try to smize at a camera it looks like I am pooping my pants and trying to pretend I am not. During my pregnancy I was more occupied with eating a whole lot of break-and-bake cookies with my husband every night while lying flat on the couch and complaining about my lightning crotch, which had me yelling out in pain every time I stood up or walked up stairs or down stairs or rolled over in bed or basically just . . . always. It always hurt.[2]

Up until now I had felt pretty okay with my identity—who I was as a youngish, married human being tromping around New

---

[2]Lightning crotch: a really terrible pregnancy issue with a really fun name. If you don't know what it is, consider yourself blessed, and I pray you will never have to experience it. If you are curious about what it is like, have a friend give you a swift kick to your lady bits every time you stand up.

York or Memphis or wherever life took us, chasing after goals and enjoying living life step by step with Kyle. But now I had to rethink an entire *new* identity for myself as a mom. Quite honestly, I was scared of becoming the sensibly dressed mom on the beach; that didn't feel like me. I was also scared of becoming an influencer-wannabe mom on Instagram—that also wasn't me. So was I even supposed to be a mom at all? Because I didn't see a lot of myself represented in that category from where I was standing: a mom who was herself and happened to also have a child. Is that possible?

Well, the pregnancy train kept rolling right along, and my fears and doubts kept chugging away all the while. Things health-wise were uneventful, and for that I was so grateful. Despite my worries and fears, I was also so excited to meet my daughter. As we got closer to the due date, I felt an ache in my stomach like I *missed* her and wanted her in my arms right that instant. And I had never even met the chick! But in that magical, wild way, I loved her more than my own life, even before she took her first breath, and I was ready to dive right into the parenting adventure and all the unknown that it would bring.

On her due date and Elvis Presley's birthday—which is a literal holiday in Memphis—my sweet baby girl was born. I will spare you the labor details, but there she was.[3] Perfect in every way.

---

[3] Forty hours. I was in labor for forty freaking hours. At the end I was so out of it I kept bumping my own leg while pushing and then apologizing because I thought it belonged to someone else. We were so loopy and exhausted, Kyle tried to pep things up and put on the Spotify playlist "Songs to Sing in the Shower"—because that makes sense—and all the nurses and doctors were dancing to Spice Girls and other nineties hits as I brought new life into the world. My daughter was born to the song "What Is Love? (Baby, Don't Hurt Me)" from *A Night at the Roxbury*. This was definitely not a part of my birth plan, but birth plans are a bunch of crap anyway. It was crazy but also awesome. Welcome to parenthood. Crazy and awesome in the most extreme ways. I hope you enjoyed that unsolicited birth tale.

In the first few hours of me holding her, she grabbed my finger and held on tight, and she felt so familiar to me. We decided to name her Sunny—or rather Kyle made the executive decision after two days of going back and forth and a nurse finally forcing us to pick something. But after labor and zero sleep, how the heck was I supposed to decide on what to name a human being? But I am so glad he went with Sunny, which was my favorite option all along; I just had no brain cells left to make a decision. So there she was, our little Sunny, and the three of us were beginning a whole new chapter of life together.

As we went home and dove into parenting, guess what happened? I stopped worrying about homely tankinis. And I also didn't worry if I wasn't living up to the standards of mommy bloggers or Instagram influencers. Now all I worried about was my precious little girl, keeping her alive and enjoying her as much as I could. Everything else became secondary, as we were completely consumed by the love we had for our child who was now earthside, and freaking adorable to boot.

There is a lot of pressure in the world. People and social media telling you what to look like, how to act. What is "normal." Well, screw all that. After having my daughter, I was happy to see that I still felt like myself—a little loud, a little weird, a lot forgetful. But I was loving and caring for her well, in my own way, and that is all that mattered.

Having Sunny and falling into my own, unique mom stride helped me realize that all women, from the Instagram model moms to the reasonable tankini moms and beyond, are amazing. And, they can do whatever they want! You—yeah, I'm talking to you—can do whatever you want. If you are being true to who you are as a woman, as a parent, and loving others well in the process, then you are succeeding. We can all benefit from keeping our eyes focused on our own lane a bit more and being true to who we are along the way, and celebrating others as they do the same. Because in doing so, you are giving other women the permission to live authentically, and you never know who around you has been looking for that kind of permission.

I am still striving to stay true to myself and working to not fall into pressures of trying to look, act, or be a certain way just because the world tells me that is how moms should be. I'm instead focusing on loving my daughter well, teaching her about God and the beautiful things of life, and making sure I don't lose myself in the process. The end. And that, I think, is parenting well. And living well, for that matter. Stay in your lane. Unfollow people who make you feel awful online. Find the people who fill you up, do what makes you happy, and put a lot of love into the world. If you do all that, you are doing all right as a mom, a woman, and a plain ol' human being.

But also, the deeper into parenthood I got, some of the mom clichés that scared me before actually became appealing. Like guys, leggings make you feel like a superhero and like you can accomplish anything, which are very helpful when caring for a small child. And I get the tankini thing—to an extent. Though I think I will settle on a nice one-piece to cover my post-baby mashed potato belly instead. Or wear whatever bikini I want and let my mashed potatoes be exposed to the universe—whatever makes me feel better that day. Pass the gravy.

CHAPTER TWENTY

SOMETIMES YOU ACCIDENTALLY HAVE A PINK THONG HANGING OUT OF YOUR SHORTS

We don't know exactly how or when God's grace will show up, but it does, unceasingly. That is something we can always count on, wait for, and expect. If you cry out to God, he will hear you. But sometimes, tangible examples of that grace and his love show up in really unexpected ways. Like one day I dropped my daughter off at daycare with a vagabond thong hanging out from the bottom of my shorts. Yes, God used a dangling pair of underwear and a large amount of embarrassment to speak to me. Life isn't boring, is it?

Here is the deal. My maternity leave was over, and Little Miss Sunshine was heading to daycare. It was a hard transition, naturally, but I felt so grateful that her school was located right across the street from our house. I would walk her to school, go nurse her on my lunch breaks, and then walk her home at the end of the day. With a few tears and hiccups along the way, I fell into my new role of "working mom" and was genuinely grateful my little lady was just a few steps away from me at all times, while still being able to work and provide for our family in the way that I needed to.

Having a baby brings on about a million new emotions and thoughts and life experiences. The easiest to see, squish, and feel is that post-baby body. I really felt it was a miracle that after having an entire human being come out of me, my body for the most part just picked back up and carried on like nothing ever happened. But even if you lose all the baby weight after pregnancy, your body is just a different shape. I found clothes didn't fit me the same way, things hung and clung differently, and I was ready to go to one of the most terrifying places a postpartum body can be: a Target dressing room. I was ready for some new clothes but knew the process of getting there would force me to stand under those horrifying fluorescent lights and look at my pale body while I tried to find clothes that made me feel more like, well, me again. But a new me. A supermom version of me, but one who still only wears cutoff jean shorts most days of the year.

Listen. I am all about an entertaining conspiracy theory every now and again, but what I am about to tell you isn't even a conspiracy. This is just straight-up truth. Target purposefully makes their dressing room lighting and mirrors the most unflattering possible so you buy everything and anything within your arms reach that makes you feel better about what you look like, and then they all laugh maniacally at us from their boardrooms as they drink green smoothies made out of dollar bills. You can go into a Target dressing room wearing your favorite outfit, full makeup and hair done, feeling pretty good, but once you glance in that cursed dressing room mirror, what you see looking back resembles Quasimodo on his worst day. But then the moment you put on their clothes, you are instantly transformed back into the belle of the ball. I don't know how they do it, but they do. Fine, take my money, Target Corporation. We all know we are powerless to your crazy marketing schemes.

So there I was. The first time in Target since having a baby, looking in that mirror that also contains the gate to retail hell, trying on all of the things to make me feel less like a lump of steamed squash and more like Titus Andromedon from *Kimmy Schmidt* in his best moment.

Because I am a creature of habit, I got all the things I usually did but in colors I didn't already own: new cutoff jean shorts that are a slightly questionable length, V-neck T-shirts, and sunglasses so big I feel I can hide from the universe in them if I so please.

This apparently has become my uniform of existence, especially since I work at home. Which is wonderful! Until the moment I actually need to meet a human being in person—you know, face-to-face and all that—for a business event. Then I am scrambling to find clothing that doesn't include frayed denim and wrinkled T-shirts.

Luckily, my eyeballs didn't burn up and fall out as I picked things out in the dressing room. I got a few new items and it felt great. Having a baby is nutso, so anything you can do after that to feel good about yourself I think is a positive thing. I went home and put on some of the stuff right away and finished out my day feeling forty points more like who I was before an alien human being decided to grow inside of me for ten months.[1]

The next day I was hurrying to get Sunny ready for school. It was one of those chaotic mornings—a fussy baby, milk to be packed,

---

[1]Not a typo. Women are actually pregnant for ten months. I don't really get the whole nine-month thing, and then we casually say forty weeks. Which is ten months! Don't shortchange me that extra month!

baby to be fed and clothed, diapers to be grabbed. All of the baby things. I was hustling to get out the door so I could get back home before I was supposed to technically be logged on to work. I saw my new clothes I had worn the night before and decided to wear them again. Even though my life felt like complete chaos, I decided it felt better to at least *appear* I had it all together. Sometimes that is enough to get you through a particularly difficult day.

I threw on the new clothes, semi-did my hair, grabbed Sunny and her bottles of milk for the day, and we began our walk to daycare. Outside it was one of those picturesque Memphis mornings. Birds singing, sunshine gleaming, calm, humid, and just perfect. I felt great.

When we got to school, the teachers all had a baby in their arms, so I did the awkward "hold your child and lean down to put the milk in the mini fridge on the floor" dance. In doing so, my butt was directly facing the rocking chairs where the ladies were sitting. When I was done, I stood up, handed my little gal over, and kissed her goodbye. I even remembered to sign the sign-in sheet that day, which I forget about fifty percent of the time, and I am convinced every daycare teacher we have ever had low-key hates me because of this. But that day I remembered, I was feeling good, rocking the mom thing, and even looking a little cute in the process. Just call me June Cleaver. That was the level of mom vibes I was feeling that day. June Freaking Cleaver.

I was happily walking back home, enjoying the beautiful weather, when I felt something hitting the back of my leg. I reached around to grab it, and my heart stopped. The moment I touched it I knew what it was, and the horror instantly flooded me.

The thong I had been wearing the night before with the shorts was still in there, hanging on for dear life as I walked around completely oblivious. And it wasn't even a subtle, nude color that perhaps would have been not all that noticeable even as it swung behind me like a cat tail. Nah. It was hot pink and lacy—because why wouldn't it be? My neon dirty underwear, flapping in the wind for the universe to see. It was dangling there when I went into daycare and bent over in front of Sunny's teachers and waltzed around like I was some hot-to-trot cool mom who was young enough to still wear too-short jean shorts and also be a responsible parent at the same time.

I don't get embarrassed very easily. But that day I was embarrassed. Beyond embarrassed, actually. That waving pink thong out of my shorts confirmed basically every mom insecurity I had, and it did so in a public way. It proved that I wasn't enough. I was too forgetful to be a good parent. Good parents would notice an extra pair of underwear sitting in their shorts before they dropped their child off at school. I was sure that I wouldn't feel cute and put together ever again. I just forfeited my right to attempt that. I tried once and found myself walking in public with a lace badge of shame waving in the wind behind me.

Buying new clothes and making small steps toward feeling good about my appearance again was just a way for me to take back some control. Because from the moment you are pregnant, you are not your own. You are bending to the will of another human being, twenty-four hours a day. And of course, when the sweet little beans are born, that only amplifies. And it is a beautiful, wonderful thing, but it is hard. And I just wanted to feel, for a moment, that I was ahead of that. I wanted to feel like myself again but also the supermom that I so yearned to be for my daughter. But there on the cracked Memphis sidewalk, crying a few tears and clutching a pink thong in my hand, I felt so defeated, anything but super, and a failure.

I walked back to my dirty townhouse, wiped my tears with my thong (just kidding—gross), and made it through my workday fine, hiding in my home behind my computer screen, completely smocked in shame. The worst part was I was going to have to walk back in there at the end of the day to pick up Sunny. Usually if something embarrassing happens you can just move on. Nope, not today. A few short hours later I would have to face the women who had a front row seat to my humiliation and channel all of Kyle's acting techniques as I pretended that I didn't have a third leg of underwear hanging out my butt just a few hours before.

I walked in, smiled, and exchanged polite pleasantries as if I had just spent the day baking organic bread for the homeless, not sobbing over a thong incident. The teachers acted normal, and I just got my little gal and began to walk home. God bless them—I will never know if they saw my thong or not, but they sure acted like they didn't. I mean, they take care of infants. I am sure most moms and dads they interact with are about one poopy diaper away from losing their minds anyway. I am sure in their teacher training they have a whole section on how to deal with sleep-deprived, stressed, and likely unbathed parents.

Sunny and I approached our house, and even though I had only been gone twenty minutes, if that, there was something on my doorstep.

It was a big bouquet of sunflowers. And an unsigned card that read: "There will be good days, and there will be bad days, but always remember that Sunny is so lucky to have you as her mom."

Are you kidding me?

I began crying, again. It seemed to be the theme for the day, so I might as well lean into it.

How, of all the days, of all the moments, did these flowers show up with the exact message I needed to hear? I didn't tell any of my friends about this, only Kyle, and he was still at work. I was racking my brain about who may have sent them, and then gasped.

Was it Sunny's teachers? Were these pity flowers?? Did they see my thong and throw me a mom bone?

It was a possibility, but I was really hoping it wasn't the case. Because while a nice gesture, that would have been the nail in my humiliation coffin. Pity flowers because they saw how much of a hot mess mother I was. Please let it not be them, and let us just go on our merry ways pretending like this incident never happened.

I began texting everyone I knew, all my gal pals, asking who did it, but one by one they all denied it.

Then I remembered my friend Caitlin. Caitlin is so calm, introspective, thoughtful, and everything I am not. But the real kicker is: she worked for the FBI. She straight up was working day in and day out fighting against local sex trafficking of minors. So basically, Caitlin was an unassuming yet powerful sneaky superhero of a woman. It had to be her.

I texted her, and her response was essentially "I can neither confirm nor deny" that it was her. Which is FBI code for "Yeah, I totally did it."

I tried to explain to her how those flowers and that message showed up at the most perfect time possible, but I don't think she fully understood. But I knew that God used her that day to give me such a tangible, physical representation of his love and his affirmation for me that I was doing okay as a mom, even though I could probably improve in the area of checking my shorts before putting them on.

It was either that or FBI Caitlin had a bug on my phone and was spying on me, so she heard me unpack my tale of underwear horror to Kyle earlier that morning and was also giving me pity flowers. I would like to hope it was God using her to show tangible love and grace. But the FBI thing is just so exciting, so who really knows.

For all of us, life can get funky and sometimes downright embarrassing. Sometimes we have days where we mess up in very public ways. Days where the false masks of "having it all together" are so clearly taken off that we are left exposed and vulnerable to the universe. But even in those moments—the bumpy, uncomfortable moments—God is there. God is working, ready to comfort, ready to show love the moment we ask him for it, no matter how much we just messed up, publicly or privately. He loves us, even when we make dumb blunders, and that is a beautiful thing.

The next time you mess up, feel like a failure, or feel less than and like you are not meeting the mark, I hope you remember my pink thong flapping in the wind behind me as I dropped my daughter off at daycare and know I am with you. And then I hope you reach out to God and keep your eyes open for his grace, like a little batch of sunflowers on your front porch, placed down in the perfect moment, in the most perfect way.

CHAPTER TWENTY-ONE

HEY—YOU CAN DO THIS!

Parenting is truly an art of being "refined by the fire." I have never experienced anything that can humble you, break you, then cause you to grow like some glorious glitter-colored phoenix all at once. The ultimate dichotomy, being a parent daily swings from being the hardest thing you have ever experienced to one of the most beautiful things you have ever experienced, sometimes within a five-minute span. Straight-up nuts is the best way to describe it, actually. I believe that is the correct scientific term.

Parents or not, we all walk through challenging times. Times when your heart and mind are so beaten down you can only conjure up the strength to utter a three-word prayer: "God, help me." Lucky for us, God hears those little prayers that come from a place of such need. And I am so grateful for that.

I experienced a three-word prayer week once when Sunny was only a few months old. Kyle was heading off to a work conference, meaning I, a new, unsteady mom with a tiny baby, was about to dive right in solo. I had known since before Sunny was born that Kyle would be taking this trip and had been dreading it ever since. And now, with her here and me still fumbling my way through this whole motherhood thing, I was really dreading it because having an infant is *hard*. It is hard when there are two of you. But one?! Seems impossible.

I have been with Kyle for so long, through so many seasons of life, I have become a bit spoiled I think. But it's not my fault! He is just so good at things and so calm all the time. I was convinced that without his strong, peaceful force in our lives, the entire house would collapse and Sunny and I—who I could already tell had a bit of my strong-willed, loud spirit—would just sit in the driveway and stare at the rubble before shrugging and going, welp, Kyle will fix it when he gets home.

Being a brand-new mom, I did call in reinforcements— Grandma. I flew my mom down to help out during our week solo. She is always so helpful and fun, and we make a great team. With her there, I was 80 percent sure we would survive. Maybe a solid 78 percent actually.

Kyle left, and we dove right in to whatever it is you do to keep a small child alive. So basically, a million things and nothing all at once. Holding, feeding, diapers, a glass of wine (for me, not baby), rinse, repeat.

But then we had a slight hiccup. And by slight, I mean massive. Two days after she arrived my mom got a fever. Then some aches, exhaustion, you know—all of the things. Girlfriend brought with her the freaking flu and was officially down for the count.

Okay, I can still do this, I lied to myself. Now not only was I solo with an infant, but I also had a germ-wielding baby boomer in my home I was responsible for. No big deal, right? Well, we all know it was A BIG DEAL.

The next day I awoke and realized that I, too, had fallen ill. Because of course I would. Of all the times to get the flu, it would be the first week I was on my own with my infant daughter.

Because life sure does adhere to the phrase "go big or go home," doesn't it.

So two of the three of us were sick. *It's okay*, I lied again. *We got this.* I reassured myself that breastmilk is a magical superfood that will provide Sunny with the perfect antibodies to protect her from this illness, and we would just shuffle along as best we could until we felt better.

Welp, the breastmilk failed me. Sunny also got a fever. Um, excuse me? I thought my magic milk was supposed to ward off all doom and destruction in our lives. La Leche League, what do you have to say for yourself?

And not only that, it was her *first* fever. And for a new parent, that is a bit horrifying. My mind was constantly racing with all the worried mom questions. Do I give her Tylenol or let her body fight it off naturally? Why is this Tylenol so purple? Is this just a food-coloring-laden toxin I am about to give her? And does she even like GRAPE for goodness' sake?! How high of a fever is too high? Should I bring her to the ER, or is the ER just a cesspool for more germs where we will all just catch another strand of the flu? Can you have two strands of the flu at once? Does she want chicken soup oh that's right she doesn't eat food so no to the soup. What do I do? WHAT IS HAPPENING?

As you can see, my brain can be fun sometimes. Especially while sleep deprived and sick.

We fumbled through our days as best we could, three generations of ladies feeling like death and having no backup reinforcements. Just us and the wild west of being sick, day after day.

The nights are when it got really tough for me. Sunny couldn't breathe out of her nose as it was stuffed up, so she was waking up a lot. One night at 11:00 p.m., as she was wailing and warm from her fever, and I was feeling like I was one wave of nausea away from barfing into oblivion, I picked her up, went into our little bathroom, shut the door, and put the shower on full blast. I stripped her down to her diaper and leaned her tiny head, the size of a grapefruit, against my chest and let the warm steam wash over us. I rocked back and forth, back and forth, and sang to her as we breathed in the warm air that was finally breaking through our sickness and giving her the relief she needed.

As I stood there, shushing her and kissing her perfect, warm little forehead, I began to cry right along with her. I felt so helpless, so weak. So defeated, with zero idea about how or when we would feel better again. About how I was going to get through the next few days until Kyle got home. And, even more, how to help my daughter. I was terrified for her, if she would be okay. It was all so new and scary. I just wanted to fix her, but I couldn't. I was not okay, she was not okay, nobody under our roof was okay, but we still had to keep moving forward anyway.

As I stood there, rocking and crying and shushing and singing, I also prayed the three-word prayer that was the only thing my soul had the strength at that time to pray. The prayer I had prayed so often before during hard times. The prayer that is small yet mighty, as it is one where we are at a place where we have nothing else holding us up but the Lord. "God, please help. God, please help. Help us, please."

The steam helped her tiny nose, and eventually Sunny quieted down and fell back asleep on my chest. I got her back into her bed before collapsing on my own. "Let the morning bring me word of your love, for I put my trust in you" was what I was repeating as I drifted off to sleep.

The next day we went through our morning routine as best we could. I was drinking my vat of coffee while getting us ready for the day. Sunny was lying on the bed looking up at the ceiling fan—the most exciting part of an infant's day—and I was attempting to get her dressed. Now, there is something you must know about Sunny. Though her name emulates all things perky and optimistic, the girl was born with a serious case of grump face. The first thing she did out of the womb was glare at me, then roll her eyes, as if saying, "Who are you, peasant woman?" But I know her. She has a sweet heart but is a strong gal who happens to have a naturally sassy resting face. It's okay—I have that as well. Too often I unintentionally look like I am mad when I'm actually fine. I've had a few people ask me what was wrong before, and it caught me completely off guard, as I was completely content, and happy even! (And if I was mad, you likely would be hearing about it because my mouth has zero filter.) But apparently my face tells a different story, and my Sunny inherited that gene. She is a happy baby, just not a smiley one. And up until this day, the only time she had "smiled" was her actually just taking a dump in her diaper, so yeah. Babies, I tell ya.

But that morning, after our night of sickness and my desperate prayers wrapped in shower steam, Sunny looked at me in the eye and smiled. For the very first time in her life, she smiled. A real smile, not a fart smile.

And I knew that tiny miracle of her first smile was the grace I prayed for. It was God's answer to my desperate prayer, to my crying out for something—anything—to help get us through the next day. I knew that, yes, things were really hard right now and they were going to continue to be for the next few days, but God was right there with me, listening to my prayers, as he had before and as he would again in the future. He was holding me up and rocking me, just like I did to Sunny the night before, quietly shushing me and wrapping me full in his love. And when I didn't feel like I could be strong, he was right there giving me his strength, just like I pour every ounce of strength into my own child.

I will never stop being amazed when I see new mercies come with the morning. That with each night that seems terrible, there is hope for a morning that can blow your flip-flops off with its goodness. I believe God's grace is able to show up. And that he listens to our cries for help. And if the situation you are walking through can't change—like when we lose loved ones or grieve something else irreversible in our life—I really think he is able to simply give us the strength to keep pushing through, which sometimes feels like a miracle in itself. And perhaps trusting in that—working to fully, deeply trust in God's love and grace and that the dawn always comes—is all we can really do. That, and try to squeeze as much joy out of our existence as possible along the way.

Becoming a "real adult" and all the growing and stretching that entails is difficult. But with a little grace, a little grit, and a never-ending resolve to keep fighting for joy, it can also be insanely beautiful. We may not ever have everything figured out, but we can try and enjoy this ride as much as possible along the way. So I hope you too will expect that grace, keep your eyes fixed on the good things around you, and enjoy this beautiful, crazy gift of life as best you can.

LOOKING BACK, LOOKING FORWARD

*T*urning thirty feels very significant and not very significant all at once. In some ways, it wraps up a really important decade full of growth, self-discovery, and likely a hearty dose of chaos. But at the same time, does anybody actually wake up on their thirtieth birthday sporting sensible yet stylish glasses, sipping black coffee calmly, feeling rested and refreshed, and blissfully congratulate themselves on finally having all this adult junk figured out as they watch the sunrise? Nah, bro. It isn't like that. Turning thirty isn't when it all starts to make sense. There is no magic age, no specific time when everyone feels completely grown up.

When I turned thirty, I was at my sister's house in Minnesota. I remember sitting at the end of her long wooden table with baby Sunny on my lap as Kyle, my parents, Jenny, and her family all sang me happy birthday. I hadn't lived near them much over the past few years, and we were rarely together during my birthday, so celebrating with them that year felt extra sweet. We drank ice-cold champagne and ate my favorite kind of cake—vanilla with vanilla frosting and rainbow sprinkles debatably unreasonable for anyone over the age of eleven.

I felt the weight of my squishy one-year-old on me and looked at the room full of people I loved, and I felt content. That's all. Content. Not like a "real adult" or finally organized or someone who definitely has their crap together both on Instagram and not, but just calmly happy. That's significant. I was content with our little celebration, with how my life had settled since becoming a parent to become more about my family, little victories, and new starting chapters. I was grateful for all the places God had brought me over the last decade, and even more so with all the people he filled it with. Twenty-year-old Katie was a far cry from thirty-year-old Katie, but also a far cry from "having it all figured out." The difference was I was okay with that. I was by no means a flawless, functioning, and responsible citizen of society, but I was proud of how far I had come. And that was enough for me at that moment.

If I looked back over my twenties, it was obvious how God was weaving everything together. Every bump, bruise, burst of laughter, and unexpected left turn brought me to this moment where I felt stronger as a woman, more at peace, and filled with joy. Perhaps that's all you can ask for. I could see how God had worked in my life, and I'm excited to see how he will continue to do so for the next decade, and then the one after that, and after that.

And I do believe he is working in your life too, person reading this. Working through your own journey, your own crazy seasons, super lame boring seasons, and ones full of so much joy you feel your head may explode into a cloud of glitter at any moment.

Life can be nuts, but also oh so sweet. And I hope that no matter what wild chapter you may be in the middle of, what decade you are trying to conquer, that you will keep your head held high and focused on the hope. Focus on the hope that yes, the hard times come, but just as sure as that, so do the good ones. Keep fighting for those good ones.

Love,

Katie

> *Hope begins in the dark, the stubborn hope that if you*
> *just show up and try to do the right thing, the dawn will*
> *come. You wait and watch and work: you don't give up.*
>
> ANNE LAMOTT

ACKNOWLEDGMENTS

Man oh man, where to begin. Thank you to every single person who was featured in this book for being a part of my life, making it better, and giving me some experiences worth writing about. Thank you to every friend I made in every single city we lived in—West Palm Beach, Austin, New York City, Memphis, and back to West Palm—for making seasons of transitions easier, better, and more fun. Each city brought a new chapter to our lives and this book, and thank you for being a part of that. Thank you to Rusty Shelton for giving me my first job in publishing, which changed my trajectory forever. Thank you to Shelby Sledge for teaching me just about everything I know about this amazing industry and PR, and being a good friend along the way. Thank you to my team at Smith Publicity for being the best coworkers a gal could ever ask for. Thank you to the Memphis Women Writers, who were the first test group for this little book and helped shape me into the writer I am today. Thank you to my agent, Rachel Kent, for taking a chance on me and giving me your amazing feedback. And to Al Hsu and the team at InterVarsity Press, for also taking a chance on me.

Thank you to my parents, sister, and amazing in-law fam, for filling my life full of good stories to tell and being a constant team of support. Thank you to Sunny and Shepherd for the endless amounts of love and joy you bring to my life. And thank you x 100, Kyle. The reasons are endless, but for this purpose I will say for always supporting me in my art, crazy goals, and dreams. I love you.

And thank you, reader friend, for joining me on my journey and reading to the very. last. word. <3

DISCUSSION QUESTIONS

1. When have you walked through a hard season of waiting?

2. What do you do when you are waiting for something that doesn't show up as quickly as you would like? How do you cope?

3. Have you ever had to make a big career or life change? What prompted that change? And what gave you the strength to make the leap?

4. Have you ever felt like God was silent toward you for a season? How did you respond or continue to have faith?

5. Have you ever felt stuck in your circumstances? What did you do about it?

6. Are you good at doing taxes? (Haha!)

7. What is something in your personality/habits you don't exactly love but have learned to give yourself a little bit of grace for?

8. How has getting older made you rethink how you were raised?

9. How has comparison to others been an issue in your life?

10. Have you had to create boundaries in a relationship—spouse, roommate, close friend—to better function together?

11. How have you experienced mental health issues? How might society better destigmatize mental illness and help those who struggle?

12. When have you had an unusual friendship surprise you in your life, like Katie and Edna?

13. How has humor helped you through difficult times of grief or loss?

14. How has God used an embarrassing moment to teach you a powerful lesson?

15. When have you felt like you were at the end of your rope but still made it through? What did that teach you about yourself? About life? About God?

ABOUT KATIE SCHNACK

Katie Schnack is a writer and book publicist. Her articles have appeared in *Relevant,* Today.com, Hello Giggles, Romper, Scary Mommy, and more. She grew up in Minnesota playing duck, duck, gray duck; learned to say "bless your heart" in Texas; lived in a four-hundred-square-foot apartment in New York City (okay, Jersey City actually, but it was close enough to Manhattan); and has a love-hate relationship with Cheetos but is also oddly obsessed with spinach smoothies. Katie and her family now live in West Palm Beach, Florida, on an acre of land with five chickens, three goats, and a senior mini pony.

For more, visit www.katieschnack.com and visit her on Instagram (@katieschnack) and Facebook (@katieschnackwriter).